FEARESSLY FREE TO BE ME

How to overcome people-pleasing in 7 simple steps

Jo Marsh is an exceptional teacher who brilliantly guides us on a journey of healing & transformation. Her signature seven steps gift us with real-world practical tools to shift our mindset and awaken our heart. Fearlessly Free is a beautiful & profound liberation for anyone seeking to take their life to the next level.

– davidji, author of Sacred Powers

Jo Marsh

BIB

Copyright © 2024

ISBN print: 978-0-7961-6732-3
ISBN ebook: 978-0-7961-6733-0
Publisher: Black Ink Books
Editing: Paula Marais
Cover design: Megan Barber Designs
Typesetting: Megan Barber Designs
Proofreading: Megan Barber Designs
Photographer team: Sven & Cheri Jurgensen.

www.jomarsh.co.za

Printed in South Africa by Print On Demand

MY DEDICATION

To the love of my life, my husband, Camel Man,
who has believed in me, in all my endeavours
and championed me when I was despondent.

Thank you for being my biggest blessing, my encouragement
and my support for one of the toughest projects
I have undertaken.

"You raise me up to more than I can be
– you are the wind beneath my wings!"

My wish for you

Tread lightly and carefully on the earth,

How you tread can heal or harm.

Speak only your truth or do not lie,

Speak clearly and kindly,

If it isn't kind, necessary or true – let it go.

Honour yourself by saying no to what does not serve you.

Be aware of your thoughts – the ones that weaken you.

Your mind is not always your friend.

Never talk about someone – it doesn't solve the problem,

Rather talk to someone and you can find a way together.

What others say is just their view and not your business,

Don't lower your vibration because others cannot raise theirs.

Waste no energy on naysayers and defending their limitations.

Your value doesn't decrease because someone else can't see it.

Listen with compassion not judgement.

Don't take things personally –

What people do reflects who they are.

Ask more and assume less,

Set intentions to avoid assumptions.

Raise awareness rather than impose expectations,

Expectations are disappointments in the making.

Take every shake up as a wake up.

Let your breakdowns become your breakthroughs

To become a more refined you.

Your time and energy are precious commodities –

Invest them wisely – avoid energy vampires and time wasters.

Thank those who have hurt you,

Bless them as your Teachers rather than curse them as your tormentors.

Follow your heart – it knows the way.

Listen to your gut – it is has all the answers.

Be all of who you are here to be –

There are no comparisons – you are unique.

Give your everything to all your endeavours –

There is no such thing as failure – only lessons.

Take calculated risks rather than live with regret.

Embrace change and fear stagnation.

Love freely with your whole heart,

It will be returned even from the unexpected.

Let heartache not make you doubt that love exists.

You can become bitter or better – you always get to choose!

Always keep dreaming,

Dreams are the seeds of manifestation.

Live without regret for what you did do – at least you lived!

Rather than live with regret for what you didn't do

And "wonder what if" or "I wish I had'.

Choose wisely how you nourish yourself with

The food you eat; the books you read; the people

You hang out with and the digital device that hooks you

Your vibe attracts your tribe!

Avoid distractions that rob you of your precious time,

Time is short and life is not promised.

Be not a prisoner of your past –

Be a pioneer of your future.

Life is not happening to you – it is happening for you.

Trust in the Divine order of life and that everything is as it should be.

Make peace with impermanence – nothing lasts forever,

Like the changing seasons and cycles of the sun and moon.

You are here as a student of life and

The lessons learnt are the fruits of your efforts.

True forgiveness is saying "thank you for the lesson" –

It sets you free!

Be kind and patient with yourself

– it's not about the mistakes you make but

What did I learn or how can I make it better?

Life is not about perfection – it's about evolution

Commune with nature and embrace silence,

It is food for the soul and where you will find inner peace.

Don't deprive those deserving of you, by shielding yourself.

Drop the coat of armour – it hides you it doesn't protect you.

Step boldly into your life – you only have this life

– it is not a dress rehearsal!

Introduction

I feel honoured that you are taking this journey with me, as you hold this book. If you are reading this, there is an inner voice already calling you to come out as your truest version of yourself. Something deep inside you has called for you to go within and ask yourself some difficult questions. As you venture through this book, you will find insights, clarity and an opportunity to reflect.

Self-worth is the essence of our being and our birthright. It is the foundation on which we build our lives as it is determined by the choices we make. It is how we perceive ourselves and the value we place on ourselves, which is influenced by many factors. These perceptions (positive and negative) are formed in the very early stages of our development and become unconscious patterns of behaviour that can sabotage our lives. That doesn't mean they cannot be changed ... they can, by first becoming aware of what is constantly showing up in your life that is not serving you, or is holding you back. This initiates the journey of transformation.

How we view ourselves directly affects the choices we make and how we live our lives. Self-worth is fragile and it can crumble when you least expect it, through any number of circumstances or situations, but especially those that involve other people. It is important that we understand, nurture and reinforce our self-worth and stand strong in who we are, when the tides of life crash against us. There is no one to rescue you, except you.

The main reason that self-worth is fragile, is that human conditioning has disempowered us through the various influences in our life.

Many people find this world a lonely place, where you

don't fit in. If you don't, the feeling you are left with is often "there must be something wrong with me". You don't feel seen or understood because you are different; or if you are sensitive then "you are emotional". You are expected to uphold family traditions, follow society norms and/or live according to others' scripts and "the right thing to do". These are the inner dialogues that conflict in us between who we are and whom we think we should be, based on our stories of the past and the people who have influenced our lives, resulting in an innate fear of being our authentic selves.

The consequence of living your life on others' terms is that you dim your own light, learn to look outside yourself and rely on others for answers, approval and direction. Few people have the clarity, confidence and courage to stand independently and fearlessly for what they believe in and who they truly are.

The majority of people fear rejection or repercussions – losing face, favour or relationships. The biggest loss, of course, is losing yourself in other people's scripts because you fall into the trap of creating a persona you think will be likeable and acceptable. You don't feel safe to share your thoughts and inner struggles (for many reasons) and the fear of standing up or standing out, is very real.

Suppressing or hiding who you are directly affects your self-worth and ultimately your overall well-being – mental, emotional and physical. Therefore it is vital for us to take ownership of our lives, find our own direction and true north, so we don't trade our individuality for conformity.

What inspired me to write this book is the commonly shared struggles and pain I have witnessed over the past two decades through the thousands of people I have coached and mentored, from graduates to CEOs in all walks of life and across industries. I, too, have walked a long and painful road wearing a mask and hiding who I am, so I could be loved and fit in … only to find out at the age of 50 that it is only the truth that sets you free. So to change your life you need to face your life.

It has become my passion to take my lessons learnt and "pay it forward," so the experiences, knowledge and insights I have gained offer comfort and inspire courage in others to awaken to the life that awaits them.

My greatest wish is to see you leap through the fire of fear, to make the changes that will shift your life from wounded to wise and worthy. This will enable you to live the life you have always wanted and truly deserve.

What I share in this book comes from my own experiences, through the "University of Life", research I have done and two decades of coaching many searching souls. I have also been fortunate to have worked with some wonderful teachers and mentors who have been my inspiration and guiding lights. In turn, my intention is to inspire you to live a truly authentic life.

My gift is to share key elements that are most commonly experienced and to offer you the space to reflect on how it relates to your life and what you discover about yourself. This will give you a starting point, clarity and focus as you embark on your journey of self-discovery.

I hope what you find helps you take ownership, stand strong in your truth and live an extraordinary life.

Your life is not a dress rehearsal. Now is the time to live the life you have longed for, dreamt of and so richly deserve.

I can say all of the above because I know that whatever has happened in my life, I am not defined by it. I get to choose what I do with it. I can be a prisoner of my past or a pioneer of my future. The choice is always mine. I can't hide from it but I can harness it and use it as a teacher rather than a tormentor to show us a better way forward, different from the one gone by. By not facing fears and the past, we perpetuate them and remain the prisoner to them. We need to allow ourselves to grieve our losses and wounds or the infection remains and it contaminates our lives through varying illnesses that subsequently arise after years of suppression.

True freedom comes from learning to embrace what happened – bad things unfortunately happen to everybody.

We cannot change what is done. However, remaining stuck in the pain or trauma is a choice and you can change that. If not, it will kill you one way or another, as it almost did me.

We all seek acceptance, approval, attention and affection. We are desperate to live fearlessly, free to be us.

Whatever struggles or traumas you are facing, I would love to help you heal your heart, find your way out of the prison of your mind and become the person you were born to be. We cannot escape the fears, mistakes, regrets and grief but, by embracing what is possible, we can escape the past.

I have shared my experiences as clearly as I can remember them, and the examples I have taken from patients' stories that reflect the core of their experiences, although I have changed all the names to protect their identity and the lives of their families.

I have also shared my winning formula: seven bold building blocks that make small changes that bring a big shift.

This is not a conventional memoir. Of course, I will share stories from my past, events that have happened, experiences that have expanded my horizons and lessons I have learnt. It's not an advice book. It's a way-of-life book based on my journey through 60 years of life. I am offering it to you as an optional lifestyle that you may like to adopt to change either your life or the way you view it. I don't believe in quick fixes like fad diets. Life is a journey not a destination; it cannot be rushed or fixed overnight.

I will share anecdotes, adventures, insights, philosophies and principles that have enabled me to get to where I am and become the person I am today. I am by no means perfect and I have not mastered this thing called Life. I have messed up; hurt people; hurt myself; made bad choices and lost opportunities. Like you, I am a student of life and still learning every day.

I am generally a cup-half-full soul. I love laughing and being playful. I have always believed in dreams. They have kept me hopeful and carried me through pain, loss, betrayal and lack of trust.

The idea of revisiting some of my life and musings was a daunting one but was driven more by the need to help others who find themselves in similar situations. This book offers the support, insights, experience and guidance to find the courage to make a decision to change where you are and heal yourself. It can be your trusted friend.

Thousands of women out there are not unlike who I have been: everything looks great on the outside, you are attractive, have a nice car, and beautiful home, travel abroad annually, are successful in a career and everyone loves you. Yet you are dying inside. Your soul is screaming silently behind the veneer about the real life you are living behind closed doors, unseen by the world and in shame of the choices you have made that have harmed you and your life.

Whom do you talk to about it that will understand and not judge you with:

"I told you so..."

"You should know better through the work you do."

"How did you allow this?"

"Why didn't you heed the warnings?"

This book culminates in a tried-and-tested road map to living life that I explored as I navigated through my challenges, and that gave me more peace and contentment, and still does. It has also changed the lives of thousands of people around the world that I have worked with as a transformation specialist and facilitator of mind-set and behaviour change.

Some of the testimonials that have come from the clients with whom I have worked:

Words fail to describe the unbelievable experience we had this weekend with Jo and her Dream Team. The transformation in everyone was astounding ... we are all so much stronger and at peace. I will never be the same again ... only better! Thank you Jo – you are a special soul – sent here to guide us all. What a privilege! Forever grateful ...

Tracy Allen

For a number of years, I have used the services of Joanne as a personal life coach professionally for work-related challenges and more recently in 2015 to provide guidance to my thought process as I travelled through the emotional "ups and downs" associated with getting divorced. During this time, Joanne has also supported me in my transition to SBV as the MD and now CEO. Joanne is a true professional who has the ability to ask very thought-provoking questions that cause you to reach deep in order to obtain a deeper understanding of yourself; I find that Joanne is incredibly intuitive and is able to read her audience exceptionally well. My experiences both professionally and privately under Joanne have been nothing short of incredible - she really is the "best of the best".

Mark Barrett

Each day, when the sun rises, right there next to us rests our road map.

Sometimes reaching out for it becomes a daunting task.

"Should I really use it or just leave it there allowing it to gather dust? Better still, why don't I just tear the bloody thing up and try something new?" reckons a little voice in your head.

There are times when certain circumstances trick us into forgetting that we all are pioneers. We, for some weird convenience, even for a fleeting moment, forget that every day we must embark on a voyage of discovery. The road map which is yours and nobody else's must never be torn or be allowed to fade under tons of dust ... The gates of this world open up once we stay true to this map.

The change in me that has been influenced by Joanne's skilful coaching has helped me realign my focus and learn to swim with crocodiles to get to the other side of the river.

Themba Khumalo

Have you ever felt stuck or in a difficult situation with work or in your personal life? I would highly recommend Joanne. She is not just your average life coach, but a "ME FINDER" and a transformation genius. She has a great deal of calmness and incredible knowledge on *how to tackle some of the most uncomfortable and difficult situations by sharing real-life examples, even some from her very own life. Her methods are simple and very clear to follow, leaving you with that A-ha moment. The best is trying out those methods for yourself, it gives you a renewed sense of confidence and impacts how you see others and how they see you. What I love most is that she approaches you with kindness and genuine care. She listens very attentively and encourages you to be mindful of the person you truly are. As she would say there is only ONE YOU!*

Humza Mahomed

PART 1

Stuck in the prison of my past

INTRODUCTION

We have just arrived at the Mother of Mushrooms. A familiar place to which Paul and I retreat when we seek clearing and clarity, and one that Tracey, my bestie, and I have frequently visited over the past 15 years. It is a warm summer's evening in March 2023 and the three of us are going on a journey to who knows where. It's an open-ended destination because Soma (psilocybin) takes you where you need to go, not where you want to go. Another adventure.

We walk into the softly lit room welcomed by the wafting fragrance of incense. I find my space for the night and settle onto my cushion as music plays alluringly in the background. I look around me in awe and gratitude of where I find myself with my own precious family – my greatest blessings:

- my loving husband, my rock and dream come true;
- my best friend and anchor; and
- my furkid Winston.

We are about to embark on a mystical journey together in which I look back on the first 60 years of my life, with insight, knowledge and rich with life's experiences. The shift from wounded to wise and worthy has been incredible. The journey was tough, traumatic and painful, yet peppered with happy moments. It was a struggle to be whom I truly wanted to be and have thankfully now embodied. I look at that young Jo and my heart breaks for a girl who wanted only the love that eluded her. She had a working mum who was always busy and never had time. She wanted to make friends but never fitted in. She was desperate to find somewhere she belonged and so, through all her efforts to gain acceptance and approval, she succumbed to the Disease to Please.

I wish I could have been her friend, to tell her she was lovable and that being different was her unique gift to the world. I would love to have been her safe place, where she could feel seen and understood and share her heart without repercussions. I wish I could have shown her how lovable she is and that she mattered in the world. I wish I could have loved her faithfully so she could believe I would never abandon her. I wish I could have held her hand as her trusted, loyal companion, as she fought for her life in so many ways, so bravely and so alone.

But we are friends today and I am grateful we have been finally reunited so we can journey on together, enriched, empowered and enjoying the fruits of our lessons.
Who would have thought this is where I would be? Free to be me. Deeply in love. With a sense of belonging. At peace with the past. Loving my life and grateful for all of it – both brutal and beautiful , with a passion to pay it forward and make a difference in the lives of others suffering the Disease to Please. I found the cure!

CHAPTER 1

I was desperate for change and now was the time. I was on top of the world – the opportunity presented itself. I had great prospects, a new adventure and was ready to leave a lifetime lived in South Africa to move to the UK. At age 44, recently divorced, I thought a complete change in my life would do me the world of good. I was a woman with chutzpah, wearing brightly coloured power suits, high heels, a mane of blonde hair and subtle make-up. I was energised by the new direction of possibility ahead. New country, new home, new friends, new job – new life!

For the first time in a number of years, I had a great opportunity to do the work I love for someone I knew and respected, who had been a client of mine, and with whom I had worked happily and successfully before. This time, in another country and in another prestigious organisation, HSBC. I needed a change and a challenge, and I thought this was the perfect answer.

I had made the most of my life even though there was a gaping hole in my heart. My people development business in Johannesburg had been thriving for almost 10 years, a number of multi-national corporates. I was facilitating workshops in leadership and management development, change management, team effectiveness and emotional intelligence, and coaching individuals on their personal growth path.

I would wake every day at 5.30 a.m. inspired to share knowledge and experience, doing the work I loved, enabling, equipping and empowering people to change their lives, and helping organisations manage change through their people. I would be suited and booted in my corporate gear and, with my bouncy energy, would hop into my convertible red Mini Cooper and head off to the conference centres to do my thing, sharing my passion with my participants.

The sessions would be abuzz with fiery confronting conversations, heartfelt truths in a safe space, shared frustrations, new ideas and plans for change. By the end, attendees would have clarity, a plan and renewed energy to go back to work and embrace their challenges with positivity and zeal. So although my energy was depleted at the end of each day my heart was full.

People would invariably arrive at my workshops despondent about their jobs; disgruntled with their teams and colleagues; sometimes even despairing of their leaders and sceptical as to what the event would fix or change. It was almost predictable. Then when they left, I would be reminded of why I did what I did when I read their sincere feedback:

"Thank you, Jo, for your time and patience to hear us."

"You inspired me by sharing your experiences and struggles, which gives me hope that I can overcome mine."

"I wish we could spend more time with you and that the rest of our team could experience what you have given us."

"I feel equipped and empowered with answers, solutions and a plan."

The feedback was what I thrived on. At the end of the day it mattered what the delegates thought. I had fulfilled my purpose and made a difference in some people's lives. This was food for my soul.

I would go home to my beloved dog, Billy, to my beautiful home and haven in Bryanston that was enough for the two of us. We would take our sunset walks daily and wind down the day with a quiet, simple evening. It was often humble soup for dinner, followed by soaking in a nurturing steamy bath and heading to bed, ready to start again the next day. Socialising and my ballroom dancing were left for the weekends.

But something was missing and something needed to change.

Here I was in my early 40s at what should have been the prime of my life, married or at least settled in a stable, loving relationship, a beautiful home and a flourishing business. That was my dream.

My life was everything but that … I had been divorced for two years and still had the burning embers of anger at myself, because I had known from the start my marriage wouldn't last. However, if I am honest with myself, there were a number of reasons why I went through with it … my need to be married and belong within a family were my drivers. My relationship with my mother was broken. We hadn't spoken in five years and I had no siblings. I was alone in the world, which left me sad and vulnerable. My friends had their own lives.

I thought that starting my life over, in a completely new place with a new career, and leaving the past behind, was the answer.

Prior to my marriage, I had been single after a number of broken engagements and was tired of hearing people say, "Why do you not have someone in your life?" or "What's a nice girl like you doing single – you should be married by now with your own family?" Everyone else around me at the time was married with their own families. The questions pressed my buttons of "What's wrong with me?" and "Why am I not worthy?", which left me feeling even more alone.

At a deeper level "approval" and being "accepted" were important to me as a "people- pleaser". Being single at 40 had the spinster stigma attached to it. So I knowingly fell into a marriage, with a man who had two children of three and five, that I knew was built on a rocky foundation. The kids and I had a wonderful bond. My mother-in-law, sister-in-law and brother-in-law all loved me. However, there were three of us in the marriage – me, my husband and his ex-wife, who controlled our life through the kids. This was never going to work, no matter how hard I tried. So we divorced after two years.

After the losses of my relationships with my mother and my marriage, and a history of attracting disastrous relationships (but at least they were relationships, I convinced myself), my Disease to Please culminated in serious weight gain. It had been a year of eating. I was a comfort eater and sought refuge in sugar. I was restless and desperately unhappy within myself, searching for the dream relationship, like a dog chasing the proverbial tyre, and yet it was eluding me. I had some wonderful friends but they had their own lives and commitments with relationships. This being my reality, I felt sad, alone and empty. All I wanted was love and inner peace. I couldn't understand why it had to be so hard to find.

Work was great but it wasn't enough. I was now fed up with people-pleasing in my life. It was taking me down a road of hollow victories and left me feeling miserable and unfulfilled. I was craving love and looking in all the wrong places. I would quietly console myself with my reliable friend, sugar – chocolate, pastries and anything with carbohydrates. Then I would loathe myself afterwards because I didn't look or feel good. It was a vicious circle.

I had read self-help books and been to various therapies and psychics hoping I would get a glimmer of hope, answers or direction. Nothing was working.

This had been going on for a year now – it was the beginning of 2006 – I was 44 and knew something had to change. I thought emigrating would do it. It would shake me up, a new challenge, new environment, new job, new home and new experiences. I had good friends in the UK who encouraged me to come over and, of course, accessibility to travel in Europe more easily with less travel time was also very appealing. What I didn't factor in was I was taking ME with me on this adventure.

So when I received the email from Mark Hamilton, a previous client in Johannesburg, that there was a position available for me to work for him at HSBC in London, and he would love to have me on his team in organisational development, it was a heaven-sent gift in answer to my prayers.

I had previously contracted to Mark and the organisation he was working for in Jo'burg for more than two years, and we had a wonderful working relationship of trust and transparency. I successfully managed a number of culture-change projects for him, which had established my credibility and built a trusted connection. He was a gentle but tall, strong man, with a quiet impactful presence. So when he moved back to the UK, we agreed that as and when a suitable position became available, he would contact me.

And so it happened six months later in July 2006: a new beginning unfolded, new life, a blank canvas on a new continent, for me and my faithful companion, Billy. We could start a new chapter and leave the others behind. In preparation I started to sell my home; sort out my life and put all my papers and documents in order; notify my clients that I was leaving and pack up to leave in four months.

August was an exciting month as I was going to the UK to iron out the details of my new role. It was also my birthday. As I landed in the UK I was confronted with the news that Hurricane Dean had swept through Mexico, particularly Mexico City and the Yucatan region, where I had made plans to swim with the dolphins in Playa del Carmen. The news said the hurricane was so bad that they closed the airport. My trip was stopped dead in its tracks. I was bitterly disappointed as a dream of many years was literally blown away. But then I thought, I am only going in a week's time so perhaps it will be over....

During my final interview, Mark, the voice of reason said, "Josey, there is usually an 'echo' that follows and you don't want to be a statistic in a country where we can't get to you. Let's not be short-sighted about these kinds of things. There will be another time. We don't want to lose you."

EARLY WARNING SIGNS – CERVICAL CANCER

In the meantime, prior to my departure for the final interview, I had received the results of my pap smear. My gynaecologist, Dmitry, gave me a concerned look, "Jo, you have early stages of cervical cancer."

I went ice cold. Hearing the C-word was everyone's worst nightmare – it's like a death sentence.

"What does that mean? How bad is it? Can we get rid of it because it's early stages?" I felt myself panicking and I could feel my heart pounding in my chest.

His calming voice prevailed and he said, "Jo it's all about early detection and then we can manage things better, before they spiral out of control."

"So what's next? What do we need to do? And how soon?" I asked anxiously.

"We will need to do laser surgery to remove it. Hopefully we can get it all out. I can't promise anything yet until we go in."

"But I am going overseas in two weeks' time. I really don't want to cancel my trip. I have so many plans that I really don't want to change …"

He immediately responded confidently, "Well, it's not spreading fast so we can wait a few weeks to do it when you return."

This was very reassuring, so we booked the surgery date for 7 September, and I left his rooms with the comfort that Dmitry would not risk anything and we had a plan. I could switch my focus to the things I was looking forward to on my trip and my travel preparation.

I have to admit that when I received the initial diagnosis, I was a little rattled. I had lost my beloved granny to cancer and was trying not to let it cloud my bright future. Fortunately, with all the excitement on the horizon, I didn't give it much airtime.

I was staying with my very dear and close friend, Antonella, in Chelsea. Though heavily overweight from her own past heartache, Antonella was a kind, strong character, a beautiful bright, smiling angel with long blonde hair, whose eyes were pools of blue and as deep as the ocean. She was also extremely talented and intelligent, an opera singer and doctor in nuclear physics. She was very much an anchor person for me and someone I trusted with my life.

She was not happy that I had even entertained going on a trip and putting my operation on hold and even more concerned that I was even considering still going to Mexico … until Mark stepped in.

Her words to me were, "Jo this has happened for a reason and you need to go home to have your operation – you can't play around with these things. You need to get it done so you can be cleared and live the life you have planned. You need to go home. Please!"

So between Mark and Antonella, a very reluctant me flew back to Jo'burg to have my procedure so that I could move forward with my life. Although I had confidence in Dmitry, I also felt a sense of dread because of the C-word and the unpredictable outcome.

When I came out of surgery, my first question was, "What's the verdict, doc"? With his usual warm, comforting smile, Dmitry said, "Good news Jo, all is cleaned out and clear, so no post-op treatment required. You just need to come back in six weeks for a routine post-op check-up. You are good to go!" I was delighted and felt an overriding sense of freedom to pursue my new life.

It was as though I had been given a get-out-of-jail pass. It set me thinking more about how I wanted to live my life – my new life without repeating the patterns of the past. I wasn't yet clear how.

I spent my recovery time looking for inspiration and direction. I found myself reading and focusing on well-known role models who were impactful in my life because of what they did to turn their lives around radically. I immersed myself in the teachings and wisdom of the likes of Dr Wayne Dyer and Louise Hay, because of how they changed their lives at the age of 60, and many others like them. I felt encouraged and inspired by their life stories and how they went from trauma to triumph and that it was possible. So if I aligned my life to the principles by which they led their lives, I would be off to a good start towards living a more fulfilled and enriched life.

I also encountered Robin Sharma and the story of how he changed his life from a high-flying attorney to a writer and inspirational speaker, immersing himself in purpose-driven living of enabling individuals and corporates in the Fortune 500 category to change their lives and organisations. By sharing some of his best practices, he offered practical ways of making incremental sustainable changes that would result in fruitful and fulfilling life-enriching change. That's what I was looking for – more purpose and meaning and some clear action steps I could take on how to live my life my way. He seemed to have a winning formula.

It was a few days after my operation that I was trawling through my personal emails, when a newsletter popped up from Robin Sharma's desk, that he would be running a conference on "Personal Mastery" in Sandton City, Johannesburg, almost on my doorstep, on 31 October.

Perfect timing and synchronicity! I thought.

I jumped at the opportunity and booked my seat. I could feel change coming and I was super excited. I had dodged a cancer bullet and was about to move to the UK, so this showed up at just the right time to help me pave a solid road to my new life.

It was a glorious spring day. New beginnings, I thought, as I went for my six-week check-up.

My gynae was happy with the outcome and I was relieved and grateful. However, there was something that had been niggling me during my recovery at home. I recalled that while lying in bed at home during the weeks that followed my surgery, when I ran my fingers over my sternum I felt an odd-shaped bump. I had had it checked out two years earlier and the mammogram came back with "dense fibrosis". I moved on and that was that. Now this same bump felt like it had grown somewhat and I was a little concerned. So I thought, while I am with Dmitry let him just check it out again.

He did a sonar scan and the frown on his face was disturbing. "There is a mass that I am uncomfortable with, and I need you to go down to pathology."

I felt the blood drain from my head. I felt nauseous. My body was tingling all over. My palms were sweating and my heart was palpitating. We looked at each other in uncomfortable silence. I headed off to the pathology lab with fear consuming me and fogging my thoughts. As I entered the pathology department, it felt cold and sterile. People were waiting to be tested, with their heads hanging into their laps surrounded by intimidating machines and equipment. Patients' cubicles were closed with bland blue curtains.

A nurse showed me to a cubicle where I met the pathologist. He was a kind man and told me he would do a deep tissue aspiration and draw a fluid sample from my left breast, which would be biopsied. When he was done, I lay waiting in the cubicle for the results for what felt like an eternity. When the doctor on duty returned, I turned to look at him with full expectation of an answer or result. He had a peculiar look on his face and wasn't making eye contact.

I touched his arm and said, "What it is?"

He said, "Jo, I am sorry. I am not in a position to give you any results or diagnosis. That's between you and your doctor."

"Just tell me if it's good or bad news." He shook his head. This was not encouraging or comforting, and my heart sank.

"I will need to spend a little more time on the sample, and I'll discuss the results with your gynae. I am sure Dmitry will give you a call next week to talk them through with you."

I went home that afternoon feeling frightened by an

overwhelming sense of doom as though I had an axe hanging over my head, waiting to fall.

I fortunately had a busy work schedule to keep my mind occupied. I also had the Robin Sharma conference to look forward to the next day. Then I was flying to the UK the following Friday to sign my letter of appointment at HSBC and look for an apartment for Billy and me.

I had lots to excite me and it helped me keep an optimistic view with the promise of a whole new life.

DAY OF DIAGNOSIS – ROBIN SHARMA

It was 31 October 2006, a sunny summer's day and I was in my element. For our country it was the end of an era – the first South African state president, Mr PW Botha, died.

But for me , it was the long awaited day for me to meet Robin Sharma – someone I had admired and aspired to be like. I dressed in vibrant red for what I felt would be a powerful day of change and was set to immerse myself in the teachings and philosophies of life from a man who modelled these teachings. He walked his talk and his example would inspire the change I was looking for in my life. My energy was abuzz. Change was in the air as I was going to get answers and actions that would help to shift my life.

I was going there for me to be inspired to be all of whom I could be by following someone who had walked his own challenging road. He had anchored his life by following sage principles with discipline, and had made the changes that brought him seemingly to a great place within himself (from adversity to opportunity), not to mention global business success. I wanted some of that.

At the 10 a.m. tea break, I saw I had a missed call. It was a familiar number. When I listened to the voice message, I went cold and my stomach did revolutions. It was my gynae's secretary with a stern message: "We have your pathology results and you need to come in."

I called her back, "Do you mean I have to come in now? I can't come now, I am at a conference. Can't you give me the results over the phone?"

"No! Doctor wants to see you today." she insisted.

My mind was racing and my heart was thumping. I was terrified by such an ominous message but angry that information about me was being withheld. I was having to sit with this anguish rather than be told on the phone.

It clearly wasn't good news so why make me wait? And I was NOT going to miss out on the rest of the day's conference after waiting so long for this opportunity. It had cost me a lot of money. So I was not going anywhere.

"It is urgent that you come in. Doctor wants to see you in person."

Due to my other commitments, the earliest we could agree to was 7:30 the next morning, before his first patient. For the rest of the afternoon a feeling of dread hung over me like a black cloud ready to burst. I now knew, more than ever before, that I needed to be at this conference and glean whatever I could to help me manage my life better or differently with whatever lay ahead.

I went home that night feeling restless. I couldn't sleep. A sense of foreboding weighed heavily on my mind and my chest felt as though a lump of lead was pressing down on it. I felt anxious with the uncertainty of what I was going to face. I was alone with my furkid and my thoughts spun as though in a tumble dryer. I wanted to call someone and talk about it to feel some solace, but what would I say? I was going through a myriad of emotions as I saw the movie of my life flashing through my mind, imagining the worst and thinking: What's next? What's going to happen to me? How will this end?

All I knew, somehow, was that I shouldn't go alone to the gynae. I also generally don't ask for help, ever. But this time I called my friend Heather. As I heard her voice, I felt my tears well up.

"Heath, I have to go to the gynae tomorrow to get pathology results. They drew fluid out of my breast on Monday and they won't give me the outcome by phone. I have no idea what to expect, I just know it's not good and I am frightened to go on my own. Please would you to go with me if you can get time off? I know it's very last minute…"

She didn't hesitate. "Jo, I'm so glad you called, you

shouldn't do this on your own. I will call my boss now and make a plan. Don't worry, I will fetch you. How are you feeling? Silly question I guess but what's going on inside you?"

"I'm scared because I don't know how bad it is. I just escaped cervical cancer and only six weeks later he says there's a mass on my left breast, and we all know what that means ..."

Heather was the voice of reason and calm during my emotional fog. She was a pillar of strength through my wobbles and turmoil.

"Jo, let's not expect the worst now, difficult as it is ... try to get some sleep, drink some chamomile tea and perhaps swallow some rescue remedy."

"Heath, I have always feared having breast cancer and, what's worse, it terrifies me to think of a mastectomy, chemo and feeling so sick with no real guarantees. I'm really scared. And I'm getting flashbacks of when my gran died of cancer and what she went through. I just don't understand, why now when I'm about to start a new life?"

"Jo, let's take it one step at a time and not jump the gun. Get some sleep and we will face the rest tomorrow, together. Big hugs my friend and just know I am with you all the way. See you at 7 a.m."

Heather was the perfect person to go with me to this daunting meeting. She is like a tall filly with a bold presence, always colourfully and snappily dressed and she moves with purpose. She's a vibrant character, with a fast wit, quick mind, challenging spirit and the strength I needed to hold my hand to hear my verdict.

The next morning, before Heather and I met the doctor, I called my client and asked if I could start the session later. I explained that the doctor had called me the day before to see me urgently. Fortunately my client, an international media house, was a longstanding one who valued and respected me and knew that this deviation in plan was not my usual style and was clearly something out of the ordinary.

"Jo, we can postpone it if necessary."

I responded gratefully, "Everyone committed long ago to this day and I cannot mess 15 people around and reschedule. I want to run the workshop. I will just start an hour later if you can keep them busy till I get there."

I tossed and turned and drifted in and out of sleep most of the night. I eventually got up at 5.30. Heather fetched me before seven and we drove in silence to the gynae. We went into Dmitry's rooms. There was an ominous air as we sat down in front of him.

"Jo, I don't know how to tell you this, I am so sorry."

"You have stage three breast cancer. I am so sorry ... you don't deserve this ... I feel awful giving you this news. I know, after your recent recovery and now this ..."

I froze from the shock. Blood drained from me and I felt lightheaded. My hands shook in my lap. I looked at Dmitry, then at Heather, in utter disbelief. Then the tears rolled down my cheeks. A sense of despair and defeat set in and I broke down into relentless sobs at the absolute injustice of it all.

"I just don't understand why or how this could happen. It's not like I live unhealthily," I wept.

Amidst my sobs Heather said. "But Jo eats healthily, she exercises regularly, she lives a clean and simple life, and she's a kind-hearted person. How? Why?"

Dmitry just shook his head, speechless, and looked down at the test results.

I managed to catch my breath and compose myself as thoughts and questions started to flood my mind.

"But I have plans, I am going to the UK tomorrow and Billy and I are moving in December. I start my new job in January."

He said, "I don't think so. You will need to do your treatment here. The costs there will be prohibitive. You have medical care and your support system here. So you will need to postpone your plans indefinitely till we see what happens."

I was stunned at what I was hearing. I couldn't believe my ears.

I felt like the bottom of my world had fallen out as more tears washed down my face.

"We will need you to see the surgeon first, and then we can decide what the next steps are, but we can do this when you come back in a week."

I was gutted, confused, angry and in denial that I had been dealt this blow. I felt like I was in a whirlpool with no way out. I had just been given a clean bill of health from the cervical cancer and now it had crept back somewhere else in my body, like a ghost that was chasing me.

Heather and I left Dmitry's rooms and stopped for coffee at the hospital shop so we could compose ourselves before I went on to run the workshop at my biggest client. I had to slow down the merry-go-round of my mind; I had to find a sense of calm so I could find some clear next steps and have a plan, while the emotions were swirling around in my heart screaming, "NO this isn't happening!"

Thank goodness for the reprieve of the workshop I had to facilitate, so I could just disconnect from this nightmare for a while. I was forced to find my centre and show up with a clear, calm head and run a full-day workshop on leadership development. Heaven only knows how and where I dug up the energy and clarity to see the day through. It was the best way I could have spent the rest of my day, focusing on how I could make other people's day better so they left the workshop on a high. It turned out to be a good day. The delegates walked out feeling empowered and inspired, their energy renewed. That high for me was short lived. I had to go home and face my future.

I knew I still had to meet the surgeon and decide on the best protocol, whatever that meant - have my surgery, and get on the road to recovery asap, however that would look. I also knew chemo wasn't an option for me, but first I had to go to the UK (my ticket was booked for the next day), undo my letter of appointment with my new boss and cancel all my wonderful plans to start my new life. I felt like I was going backwards, fuelled by the agony of letting go of this new beginning I had longed for. It was now beyond my grasp. I felt robbed of a promised future.

THE NEXT THREE DAYS – MY INNER WAR

My inner war was raging. I needed to make clear, responsible decisions that would set the trajectory for the rest of my life. Like an unreasonable irrational teenager, I was furious that my life was being restricted AGAIN. I cried, sometimes uncontrollably, as if someone had died. I have never felt so alone and so scared. I had no family, no partner or husband to console me or talk things through with me, let alone comfort me. The C-word felt like a death sentence. My thoughts and emotions were all over the place like a bucket of frogs. I had just been given a clean bill of health from my cervical cancer when the Universe seemed to be saying, "Oh no, we are not done with you, you have another rodeo to go."

Now here I was again. I couldn't believe the injustice of it all. Why? Why me? What had I done to deserve this? I didn't deserve this? Was this some sort of karmic debt? My plans were being screwed up for my new life and, worst of all, the echo of my deepest fears (since my early teens) rang loud in my ears: "Please God don't let me be a divorcee and please don't let me get breast cancer." I couldn't understand why I was being punished with the two things I so wanted to avoid in my life.

I went through the entire spectrum of emotions and questions, and was gutted that I had to cancel all my plans to move to the UK. Why now?

I had to gain some control and have a plan. So Step 1 was to go to the UK and close that future chapter for now and process what I had to face. Then in Step 2, on my return, I needed to meet the surgeon, talk about my options and come to a decision about the way forward as that would determine my steps to follow.

I woke up on Friday morning as though emerging from a nightmare. Only this wasn't just a nightmare. It was my current reality. I had to meet Mark, break the news and face the disappointment of letting go what I was so anticipating I could not take the job. However, time with my precious friend, Antonella, would be comforting medicine for my soul and I could rely on her wisdom, absorb her compassion and be encouraged by her clear thinking. She really was an anchor in my life and I trusted that she would help me process this all and find some clarity, and maybe some answers and direction.

A-HA DAY – A WHOLE NEW WORLD OPENED
BY DR CHRISTIANE NORTHRUP

On the flight to the UK I kept asking myself when this all would change, this constant uphill battle to find peace and love.

Something had to change. I was desperate and dying inside.

When I arrived in London I felt I could let my defences down a little, as I was now safely with my trusted Antonella. She was intelligent, wise, intuitive, compassionate, insightful and spiritual, and I felt safe to open my heart to her. She totally got me. She was a pillar of strength and a source of comfort and solace while I was trying to decipher the myriad emotions between my tears of fear, despair and anger at the injustice of what I had to face. My mind was reeling and my body was rebelling at the thought of a possible mastectomy and chemo – my worst nightmare. Amidst my wailing tears I spewed to Antonella, "What's going to happen to me? Is this how my life ends?"

I was searching for hope.

Antonella stood up and said boldly, "Right, that's it, we are going to Waterstones to buy you a book you MUST read. There's a profound work I think might help you make sense of things and clarify your choices. Let's go!"

I had no clue what she was talking about. I just knew it would be something positive and constructive in this mess. She took me to Waterstones bookshop in Piccadilly to buy me the book that started the REAL change I NEEDED and not the one I was looking for by moving to the UK. It was Women's Bodies, Women's Wisdom by Dr Christiane Northrup.

With book in hand, a hint of hope and renewed energy, we headed off to Carlucci's in South Kensington to delve into this tome over a coffee so I could understand more about what I was facing and how to navigate through it. It was an eye-opener for sure and far too much to digest in one sitting. This was going to be my companion on my flight home to SA.

After meeting Mark and withdrawing from my job, I left. It was bittersweet saying farewell to Antonella, and an opportunity lost.

"You are a gutsy girl Jo and taking bold steps. I am cheering you on every step of the way. You are making the right decision, just limit whom you tell, as not everyone will buy into it because of their own fears and perhaps lack of knowledge. You don't need to be derailed by other people's opinions. So stay focused, I am behind you. You can do this!"

Her words gave me confidence. Even though her background was in science, she was totally supportive of my decision to sidestep the conventional path prescribed by the medical fraternity, as it would not heal the wounds that caused the disease in the first place. After all, I'd had two diagnoses in quick succession and I was the common factor. Therein lay the clue and the message.

On my way to the airport, I was reflecting on this particular trip. It was quite surreal, as travel has always represented an adventure of some sort or was business related, yet this time it was everything but that. I had a sinking feeling of going home and ultimately facing the road ahead alone. I had no idea how my life was going to unfold.

Yet, somehow I felt lighter in my heart than when I had arrived in the UK. I was feeling more empowered, with a new-found understanding that I had more choices than I thought I had, all clearly outlined in the blurb at the back of the magic book. This gave me hope. I could take charge of my life, take the next steps on my terms and not succumb to others' imposed directions. I was also making a decision to change my life the right way around – from the inside out. Healing the heart wounds would heal the bodily wounds. This would ultimately be more sustainable and more honest, than constantly seeking joy outside (which is a BAND AID) and hoping it would fill the hole inside.

My journey home was a rollercoaster ride of emotions and sadness at the loss of a wonderful opportunity for a new life. The plan for my future was now unknown. I was scared and there were no guarantees. What a mess! I needed to make real changes within me. What did that all mean and require? I also needed to accept the fact that everything happens for a reason as unclear as it was, and that my life had been brought to a halt for me to pause, reflect and redirect it.

With that, I took that huge book out of my bag and decided to stop the swirl of destructive thoughts and make better use of my time in this confined space till I landed in Johannesburg.

I flicked through the pages. There was so much information. I was overwhelmed. I was battling to concentrate and feeling restless. I read the same lines over and over again and absorbed nothing. I walked up and down the aisle to settle my nerves and watched my fellow travellers immersing themselves in films, books or laptops, while others slept. I certainly couldn't sleep, and movies couldn't distract me. All my mind would entertain were the fearful prospects as I played out all the ways the road ahead could unfold.

I knew I had to change my life and the type of choices I was making. But I knew for that to happen that something had to change inside me. I couldn't keep finding myself in the same situations and recycling the same patterns in response to them. I was always afraid of speaking what was true for me or to stand up for what I wanted, because there was invariably some form of inflammatory backlash and I hated conflict. It was making me sick and I couldn't do that to myself again. I was being given a second chance to recover fully from two rounds of cancer. I couldn't allow myself to recycle the same patterns that would result in the same experiences or situation. I was clearly sick of it or getting sick from it. It needed to change.

Before landing in Jo'burg I made a final attempt to find at least one insightful gem in the book. I read that every physical illness has an emotional root cause. This was my a-ha moment. I realised I had work to do.

I arrived home exhausted from the emotional churn throughout my trip. I had to put that behind me and focus on the situation at hand. It was a huge comfort knowing I had the loving support of friends who walked alongside me. However, I was still alone with my thoughts and decisions and their consequences. I was scared.

The next day I had to ready myself to meet the surgeon to discuss treatment options. I called my Rock of Gibraltar, Heather, for support. She said, "I'll fetch you. We're in this together."

On the walk to the surgeon's office, I felt as if I was going to hear my sentence passed. His office was cold and stark, white with walls barren except for his medical certificates.

The surgeon was cordial and went straight to the point. Clinically, he began by downloading the list of steps to be taken, like a shopping list. The longer the list went on the more anxious I became.

"I will have to do a bilateral double mastectomy." That sent my mind reeling and my eyes were like saucers in horror.

"I will have to induce menopause." I thought I was hearing things and my mouth dropped. (I am not usually at a loss for words).

"I will have to give you beta blockers and I will then start chemo and radiation."

As I was listening, my tears fell uncontrollably.

He continued, "You will then have to go on Tamoxifen for five years and a maintenance regimen of HRT thereafter."

This was like a horror movie. I felt I was drowning in his prescription. The thought of losing one breast was terrifying enough but losing both was horrific. Not to mention the loss of a woman's symbol of femininity and dignity. In a shaky, frightened voice I asked, "Why do I need to have both breasts removed?"

"Statistics show the cancer could spread to the second breast and best practice dictates that it is safer to remove them both. It will be a matter of time before we have to deal with the other one. We might as well remove it now."

The wind was completely taken out of my sails and it felt like a blow to my solar plexus. One breast is malignant not two, so how does one lead to another? A nagging voice inside me questioned this download of medical solutions. "Is this the only way – surely not?" I asked myself.

Loud alarm bells sounded in my head that we needed not act in haste. I was terrified of making a mistake by just reacting to what was prescribed without having time to process and digest it all. My decision had to be one I would not regret.

This conversation was galloping downhill fast. It was time for me to gather my thoughts and process what I had just been told. I was overwhelmed and couldn't think clearly. Fear was enveloping me at the prospects. What if I made the wrong decision? I asked one final question through my tears, "I respect you have a medical protocol to follow but surely there must be another alternative so I can also have a choice?"

The surgeon looked up at me over his glasses and said matter-of-factly. "Then we must remove at least the left breast, but I can't be responsible when the cancer shows up in the other one..."

Heather and I looked at each other in shock and disbelief at what we were hearing. This was no consolation. I was mortified at the thought of removing either of my breasts. I was about to excuse myself and leave. But I stopped and asked slowly, "And is there a third option?"

"Not really, but the bare minimum is to do a lumpectomy with no guarantee of success."

"I'm happy with that," I responded.

He nodded unemotionally. "I will look at my theatre roster, confer with the plastic surgeon and my assistant will contact you later today to give you my earliest slot next week."

After that tumultuous meeting and wrestling with the options of which route to go, I left for the plastic surgeon who was going to be assisting in part of the procedure for partial reconstruction. I coincidently knew him personally – the brother of an old school friend. This was a different meeting altogether. Although he provided solutions that, as a doctor, he was obliged to recommend according to the Hippocratic Oath and the standard medical protocols, he was more open to my questions, collaborative and compassionate. He was empathetic to what I was facing and what was important to me. He also respected what I wanted to follow on my healing path. He promised to do his part in theatre and support my choices. I felt comforted and safe to take the next step and move forward with my lumpectomy, satisfied that he had my back in theatre.

Processing that night the discussions I had had with the professional team, I felt overwhelmed and anxious. Surgery was only a few days away but it was a long wait to be rid of this torturous tumour. I took time to consider all the information from the discussion in the surgeon's rooms. Why did I feel so rattled and unsafe with his mastectomy regimen? I picked up the book again to see if I could find answers and hopefully some consolation.

I found that Women's Bodies, Women's Wisdom powerfully illustrated that when women change the basic conditions of their lives that lead to health problems, they heal faster, more completely and with far fewer medical interventions. Dr Northrup explained the workings of the female body in an accessible way with a guide through a comprehensive list of women's conditions and concerns like menstruation, pregnancy, fibroids and menopause, to name a few. She also showed you how to heal yourself by listening to your intuition and your body's innate wisdom. She combined the best of both contemporary Western medicine and natural remedies and Eastern healing philosophy along with the body's own miraculous healing powers.

I explored further to understand the root cause of my original cervical cancer and my current diagnosis.

The answers were alarmingly accurate and insightful:

- The root of my cervical cancer was physical abuse and neglect as a child, resulting in power/control issues with and by other people.
- The root of my breast cancer was unresolved emotional hurts and resentment from the past due to lack of love; giving everything to get love; and fear of abandonment.

Bingo! I was in awe of the accuracy. It sounded like the real diagnosis. The cancer was just the outer manifestation of all that had been buried in my body for so many years. This made more sense to me and I could start to digest my situation more easily. I felt more empowered with this information and more confident in my decision. Suddenly my agitated gut was calming. Both my grandparents had been pharmacists and traditional medicine was the norm. As I grew up my mother was always at the doctor for something or other and had been through multiple operations without hesitation or questions to the doctors. Some were successful and some were not. It was the unsuccessful ones that left me not wanting to put my life in someone else's hands without taking some responsibility myself.

I have always known cancer is a silent killer. Yet after the trauma of diagnosis, I now understood the long-term prognosis that stress and suppressed unresolved emotions were at the core of it. I needed to clean up my act and make some dramatic changes to my inner landscape.

I didn't know where to begin to glue the pieces of my life together again, in spite of all the coaching skills I had gleaned over the years, personal development I had coached and soul searching I had done. I had no clear view of where to from here.

Dr Northrup's book became my healing bible and cemented my decision on what my healing road would look like. It didn't include any of the things the surgeon had in mind for me. I chose to have a lumpectomy to remove the tumour followed by radiation to cauterise the area for safety's sake and prevention – but that was as far as I was prepared to go with medical science. The rest was up to me, much to the disapproval of the surgeon and the oncologist. They told me, "You are totally irresponsible," which was echoed by my mother who disapprovingly said, "You and your fancy ideas, what makes you think you know better than the doctor? It's actually reckless and selfish."

I responded that it was my body, my life and my choice, and I was happy to bear the consequences. This was always where Mom and I came unhinged. One thing I knew for sure, and was evident in this conversation, was that if I did something of my own choice and made my own decisions, it would often come with some form of disapproval or criticism from my mother. It was no different this time … but I remained unshakable in my resolve, without fear of conflict or some sort of repercussion.

The muddy waters of my confusion became clear. Being swayed any other way was not an option. THAT was when my journey of healing began. The changes in my life unfolded from there. I found my voice and fearlessly stood up for me.

This a-ha moment opened a window of hope and sent me searching for more understanding, not so much of what I had done to get me into this situation, but how to change it, so I could let it go and move forward with my life.

It was a bit like an adventure into the unknown but this was about my life. It was about choosing a direction for my recovery path and being okay with whichever way it turned out.

This odyssey was both scary and exciting because I stood alone in my choices and consequences. Yet, somehow, I felt empowered and knew it would be better in the end. For the first time, it would be on my terms, and I could live with that in spite of any naysayers.

I finally understood that, actually, change is an inside-out job, not an outside-in job. I was looking for a better life outside of me when it needed to start inside of me. By going to the UK I was taking me with me – it couldn't be left behind, as I had thought. So it was time to face my life, take back the driver's seat and no longer be the passenger. This was not going to be a quick fix or cured by a doctor. I had to heal me causally and the doctor would treat me symptomatically. This was the turning point where I suddenly felt a spark of confidence.

I felt lighter and was deeply grateful to Antonella for the gift of time with her and this magical book. What a rewarding trip my flight to London had been. This new-found information gave me a sense of empowerment and an answer to the mystery of why this happened. I could finally make peace with it and start to work on the solution rather than drowning in the problem. I had felt powerless and scared at the mercy of others, including the doctors. This was my lifeline and I was so grateful.

All I knew was that I had to listen to my gut and follow my heart in spite of outside resistance. It was the only way. The feeling was particularly strong. I feared more the regret I might feel if I didn't follow my truth. Now, I had some internal housekeeping to do – cleaning up and cleaning out. I needed to make the right decisions for me, not the ones I felt pressured into making by the doctors, or by anybody else for that matter. I needed to be unemotionally careful and responsible so I could feel at peace with whatever the consequences.

I was suddenly feeling optimistic and more confident. I knew whatever the surgeon said, chemo was never going to be an option for me. I felt strongly that it would harm me more than heal me. This was also suggested in the book. Healing was the work I had to do without pills, potions, drips or toxic chemicals.

Dr Northrup highlighted repeatedly that every illness is the outer manifestation of emotional roots seated in unresolved trauma. I also understood that it was my responsibility to rewrite my biography and thereby change my biology. This felt like a huge mountain but one that I was determined to summit. There was no way out but through.

So where should I begin and how? I needed to stand

strong in my resolve and not swerve in any form of adversity. It would not be a quick fix but it would have long-lasting results.

My journey had now begun with my decision to work on me and heal me.

MY MOTHER ARRIVES BACK

The morning before my operation one of my close friends called me. Christine had been a long-standing friend – a Greek mama personality who loved to nurture and mother people, including me. She took my diagnosis badly. She was devastated and wanted to do something to fix this whole painful situation and wanted what she thought was best for me.

"Jo, how are you feeling about your op tomorrow?"

"I just want it over with so I can move on."

"Are you comfortable and confident with your decision not to go through with the mastectomy and chemo?"

"I have never been more sure, especially after it being substantiated for me in Dr Northrup's book. I know this is the right way for me."

"Joey, I know it's your decision at the end of the day. I just hope it all goes the way you want it to. It's just a bit unnerving for me because we don't know how it will go."

"Chrissie, it's what I can live with. The thought of chemo and loss of dignity on so many levels, not to mention months of vomiting and hair loss and all the other complications that come with it and how it can affect other organs, is too much. What flaws me is that they guarantee me only five years by going the chemo route. What will my quality of life be? So I would rather go with my choice and live a shorter, quality life if that is the way it is meant to be, but my dignity will be intact."

Not convinced she enquired, "Okay, but because you have chosen the unconventional way, wouldn't it be the right thing to let your mom know you have cancer?"

"Why? She can't be part of my life when I am well, why would I want her there when I am ill, especially as she is part of the pain that caused it?"

"Well, we don't know how the dice are going to fall and if the unthinkable happens, then what?"

"That's life isn't it? I really don't need or want her in my life right now, given our history."

"Jo, I can call her if you don't want to, but she needs to be told – it's only fair."

"What she did is not fair and clearly she hasn't missed me, so what can of worms are we opening?"

As we debated the pros and cons of telling my mother the news, I had a flashback to a dark night of the soul 10 years before, caused by my mother. It was a time when I felt totally alone, lost, powerless, not understood, not good enough and craving love.

I decided to share this with my friend, so she would understand why I was reluctant to have my mother at my bedside. "Chrissie, let me share with you why I don't feel safe sharing this news with my mother."

"I had just gone through a brutal betrayal by a long-distance boyfriend I had dated for five years. A telefax was forwarded to me by his head office in Germany, from someone I did not know, and it said, 'Heinz, where are you? I have been looking for you for three weeks and our baby is due next week?'"

My blood ran cold and a surge of anger rippled through my body so that I started to shake. It was during the time that I questioned working in the same business as my mother because I didn't have a life. I had no personal freedom. Everything was governed by my mother, including the finances. I had zero individual power or independence. Whatever I did was never enough or good enough.

So with a broken heart and a mother who was emotionally unavailable to me I felt desperately alone. The best she could offer me in this horrific situation was, "Well, he was a bit of a dark horse you know" and "Long-distance relationships never work."

Yet she supported the relationship. My emotions were

raw and I didn't know where to turn for comfort. I just couldn't see my way clear to any freedom. I kept asking myself, "Why is real love so hard to find? I am not asking for a lot, so what am I doing wrong?" I was on an emotional downward spiral and I knew I needed to talk to someone objective who could help me get clarity, direction and know that I was not abnormal. I came up with an idea and approached my mother. "Mom, I am drowning in my emotions. I feel sad all the time and I can't get through a day without crying. Do you think I could find a therapist, someone impartial I can talk to about my feelings and what I am going through? Maybe they can help me clear my thoughts and emotions."

She turned to look at me down her nose through her glasses with disapproval and said, "We don't do mental cripples in this family, Joanne. So pull yourself together and get on with life. We all have problems and have to deal with them. We don't have time for this nonsense."

I was dumbstruck and felt completely hopeless and helpless. Disheartened and dejected, I thought: Where to from here? I have no one to turn to. No family to turn to, no siblings and no real close friends I can trust with my desperation. I felt isolated in my pain. I eventually decided there was no way out but out. If this was going to be my life for the rest of my life, I wanted out. I needed a fail-safe plan so I could be confident my end would be error free. I chose the day carefully. It was a Friday afternoon. Our secretary went off at lunch time. Our housekeeper, my nanny when I was little, had the day off. My mother was out with friends. It was the perfect day and I was prepared.

I went to the garage, attached a hosepipe securely into the exhaust of my red Mazda and closed all the doors, with my dogs safely out of the way. I couldn't say goodbye to them. I needed to finish this quickly and efficiently before anyone came home and could stop me, and before I lost my nerve. I left no note. I sat in my car shaking, with my heart pounding. With the hosepipe through a gap in the window, I closed the door. Thoughts raced through my mind as the fumes filled the car, starting to make me nauseous. This is it; this is what my life has come to; sad and alone; who would care anyway? At least I will be with my dad and granny. The nausea worsened and I began to feel light-headed as though I was going to pass out. I steadied my breath so as not to panic. Through the haziness, I vaguely heard a tapping or scratching near me and I couldn't figure out what it was. It was incessant but I didn't want to move as I would have to start again and would perhaps lose my nerve.

This scratching was relentless. Then a thought came to me: somebody has come home. I panicked and turned off the engine. I opened my car door and, as I put my foot down to get out, I stumbled and I put out my hand to break the fall. I felt a tongue licking me with vigour – it was my poodle, Snoopy. He was climbing all over me, licking my face as if to wake me and I wept into his fur. That kind of love did not deserve me deserting him and, with his persistent scratching on my car door, was more determined than ever to keep me alive. He saved my life and he was worth living for. He must have sensed something was afoot and somehow worked the sliding door open from the garden side with his nose and his paws. There was later evidence of scratch marks on the wooden door. I knew from that moment as he and I cuddled into one another like lost friends that I had to find another way. I couldn't leave my best friend like that. I couldn't take my life and abandon my best friend and faithful companion.

Christine responded with a logical suggestion. "Jo, let's just do the right thing and give her the information. What she does with it is up to her. She deserves to know – she's your mother. It doesn't have to change any decisions you have made. Though I feel shaky about your plan. I am behind you every step. You have made an informed decision based on your research and intuition. I trust you because you are making a conscious choice after weighing up the options."

I was too tired to argue and gave up.

The day came for my lumpectomy. It felt surreal. I was going in for an op that people talked about but I never imagined I would need. I was worried less about the operation per se, and more about what I would hear afterwards. Would it be worse than or better than we knew? I deeply hoped it would be the latter. A friend fetched me early, took me to hospital and waited with me till I had to go to theatre.

Everything happened so quickly. I hardly had any time to think about the operation. I was checked in and given a theatre gown to put on, my blood pressure and temperature were measured, and the anaesthetist gave me my pre-op relaxant.

It was just minutes before the theatre nurses came to fetch me from my ward. I was in the hospital bed prepped to go into theatre, three of my girlfriends were with me to hold my hand and wish me well. And then, unannounced, my mother walked in.

I hadn't seen her in four years. We hadn't spoken to each other since my 40th birthday in 2003. It was a shock to see her and, as if the anxiety of the imminent op wasn't enough, the flood of emotions that washed over me was overwhelming. I burst into tears as she approached my bed. I felt so small, frightened, confused and vulnerable. Through my sobs, I could garble no more than, "I love you, Mom."

She responded with a pat on the hand, "You will be fine, Joanne, millions of women go through this and survive and so will you."

That dried my tears very quickly. I went from "Wow, my mom is here to see me" to "fucking bitch, what the fuck?" within minutes. Dismissive and diminishing again. Is that why she came? Why did she bother?

With that the nurses arrived and I was wheeled away to theatre in a sea of emotions. I was wrestling between the shock of her showing up and the anger at her hard-core insensitivity at a time like this. She had no idea what I was feeling. Nothing had changed even at a time like this. She was a piece of work and to put her and the word 'mother' in the same sentence was unthinkable.

What would it have taken to show some compassion like, "Jo, I will be here for you when you come around and let's take it one step at a time. I know it must frightening," which would have been more comforting.

I was jolted back to reality when I found myself under the big theatre lights with the distinct smell of ether in my nose. Nurses asked me to slide onto the operating table. I was grateful to see the warm familiar face of Dmitry and the plastic surgeon. Then the anaesthetist appeared at my bedside with his loaded needle. I was somehow thankful that I could escape into an induced sleep, and could shut down those hurtful thoughts and memories that flooded my mind uninvited. What I was facing now was a battle I was determined to win. For the first time in my life I was not about to let anyone, let alone my mother, derail me.

THE FIGHT WAS ON

Something strange happened between the time I was wheeled away to theatre and when I found myself back in my ward after the operation. I saw the warm, smiling and relieved faces of my friends around my bed and felt loved and cared for. Although I was drowsy, I was very awake. An inner fire was blazing in my chest and belly; my mind was racing at the realisation of where I was and why I was there. I knew I needed to get out of the hospital as soon as I could, to go home and recover alone and on my own terms. I was on a mission to heal myself and no one was going to stop me.

I remembered my mother coming to see me and it felt like more of the same from years gone by. I didn't need to combat that as well as the dreaded lurgy, especially as they were inextricably intertwined. She really didn't get me and her approach to life was far removed from mine. Many a time I would ponder on how I could even be her daughter, so vastly different were we. One obvious relevant example of that was, whenever she was ill or in pain, her first stop was a pill, potion or operation, and she would never take responsibility for her own health. It was always "that's the doctors' job". So already the gap between my way of thinking and my mom's was worlds apart.

This recollection fuelled my determination to be out of the hospital. If I could have my way, I was not under any circumstances staying for the prescribed three-to-four days. I was going home the next day, come hell or high water. And so I did.

The next day was a gloriously sunny Saturday. Heather arrived to see me.

"Wow, you look amazing considering you had four hours of surgery less than 24 hours ago."

"I feel good, Heath, and somehow lighter."

"Jo, you look as though a weight has been taken off your shoulders."

"Strangely enough, I feel different and better knowing the tumour is out, whether it is psychological or not."

We went outside and sat under the trees to enjoy the sun and fresh air. I was waiting for the plastic surgeon to visit me so I could ask to be discharged.

Heather and I talked through my options. I shared with her what I had discovered in my new health bible, and I was comforted by her support of my decision. Healing at home was the first step.

The doctor arrived while Heather was there. He looked at me, smiled and said, "Well aren't you chirpy and cheerful?"

I responded, "Well, I'm ready to go home" with some chutzpah in my voice.

With wide eyes he said, "But …"

"Doc, the bad guy is out now and I really want and need the peace and tranquillity of my home and haven. That's where I will get better. I can sit in my own garden and be comfortable in my own space with my Billy boy. I promise to go gently, to do all the right things and rest. I just don't want be surrounded by ill people for the next four days. I also don't want to endure the pressure of others' opinions and the obligation of listening to people's fear-based advice that could take me off my course."

He rolled his eyes at me and said, "Jo, only if you promise to not go out and about and think you are a rock star. You have had four hours of tricky surgery so don't do anything silly."

"I promise you with all my heart – it is that important to me. I just desperately need silence to be with my thoughts. My recovery and wellness are my highest priorities. I need this time, so I can arrive at a place where I have an unshakable clarity and calm with a plan on how I will take better care of my well-being. Staying here makes me feel anxious."

He conceded with a knowing look. "I will sign your

discharge card. Please collect your script from the pharmacy. And I want to see you in my rooms on Tuesday. So please arrange for someone to drive you."

I wanted to leap out of the bed I was so overjoyed and grateful. He hugged me and left.

Heather and I wasted no time. We packed up and were out of there.

I got home with my heart overflowing with joy to be back with my Billy boy, who was wagging every part of his body when he saw me. I felt relief and safe in our sanctuary. This was where my healing began.

PART 2
Changed tack – failed

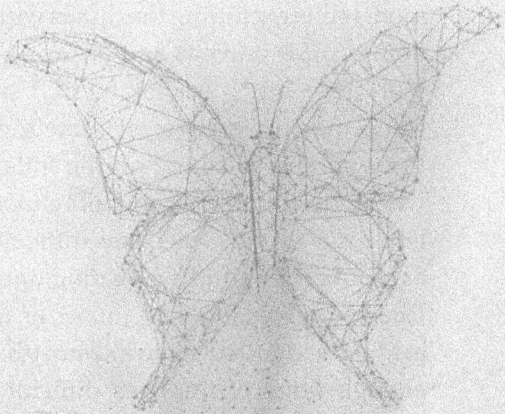

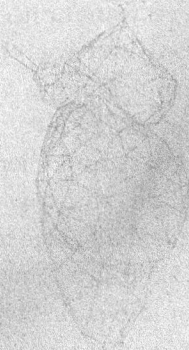

MY INSIDE-OUT JOB (DETOX AND DIET)

As the weeks went by, I was feeling better and better. I was enjoying this time out to just be, rest and reflect. I was definitely recovering well. As part of the process I was on a mission to clean myself up from the inside. That meant physically and practically as well as mentally and emotionally. However, I did it step-by-step starting with physical practicalities like diet, sleep, being outside in nature and supporting my healthy healing with the right supplements. I was juicing daily with fresh fruit and vegetables to nourish my body with raw natural food, while excluding the things with the highest sugar content, doing coffee enemas and ensuring I was alkalising my body with the foods I was taking in. I stuck to fish and free-range chicken as my sources of protein and let go of all red meat. I put an end to eating all the inflammatory foods like dairy, wheat, carbohydrates and all refined sugar. Reluctantly I even let go most fruit (which was difficult as I LOVE summer fruits) except berries and I was eating only green vegetables. I knew I had to lower my acid intake or anything that converted to acid once ingested, even alcohol (that wasn't difficult). Funnily enough none of this was difficult and I realised that when you have a strong WHY you want or need to do something, it becomes easier to do. My only vice was coffee. It's a daily ritual for me and has many meanings to me. Chemo would kill me before coffee did, was my thinking.

I now needed to hop over another little hurdle. It was six weeks after my operation, which was successful and the wound healed well. The time had come for the obligatory visit to the oncologist (which I did grudgingly but went through the motions, if only out of idle curiosity). It was either going to confirm why I didn't want to have chemo or shift my thinking completely. So I went, knowing I had nothing to lose and I didn't have to commit to anything I didn't want. I knew I needed to make an informed decision from a place of self-empowerment and take full responsibility for it.

As I walked to the oncologist's office, I passed a line of about 12 chairs, all occupied by patients with needles in their arms and a drip hanging beside each of them. Some looked worse than others. Most had no hair and looked like ghosts, grey or yellow in pallor and appearing very unwell. I felt my stomach churn with nausea. I made my final decision right there that I was not going to be one of them.

I made my way into the doctor's office. He already looked foreboding, which left me feeling uncomfortable. It was a jaw-dropping experience. He clearly had his plan and protocol of standard practice and was clinical and matter-of-fact in his approach, which was unsettling. It was probably the most scary part of the whole experience for me because of the dreaded side effects. I was looking for comfort and compassion. He was just doing his job.

When I found my words, I asked him, "What about the side effects and long-terms effects?"

He seemed annoyed at my question, evident in the way he dismissively rattled off his reflex answer, "What kind of a question is that? Everything has side effects but do you want to live or die?" That was not comforting at all and I was feeling very anxious. I was really trying not to be provocative but, much like it had been with the surgeon, I needed to feel that I had a say in my own road to recovery and to achieve some peace of mind in what was already a scary ordeal.

The final blow was when I asked him, "How much life can you guarantee me with this protocol?"

He pragmatically answered, "Well, there are no guarantees in life." What an answer when death is staring you in the face. I guessed he had had to distance himself from all the years of treating cancer patients and all their emotions.

I felt the tears well up in my eyes. I was seeking solace and tentatively responded. "A mechanic guarantees his workmanship on a car... I need a more comforting answer."

He was clearly frustrated with me and without looking at me reluctantly said, "Five years."

I looked at him in horror that he could say that so flippantly when we were talking about LIFE, not a car battery. I was even more convinced now that this was not going to part of my healing journey. I was just getting more and more anxious. His sterile manner and lack of kindness left me feeling very guarded. It confirmed my decision about how I wanted to restore my health and well-being.

"Then I will rather do five years my way. At least my way I can have quality of life, rather than vomiting daily, losing my hair, my appetite and my dignity, being anaemic, having a wasted immune system, sores in my mouth so I can't eat, bruising and bleeding, nails going black and feeling half dead and probably dying anyway."

He shrugged indifferently and before the conversation could go any further, I picked up my bag, turned on my heels and left. He called after me, "We aren't finished ..."

"I AM!" I called back, briskly walking down the gloomy passage past the line of sad, ill faces. This depressing image embedded my decision. "I would rather die than have chemo and go through the torture that these people are enduring."

His receptionist, wide-eyed and alarmed at the heated exchange, could see I was upset. I'm sure she was used to that. "Before you leave, the doctor needs you to please sign this indemnity form."

"What is it for? I'm done here."

"It just says doctor is not responsible for your decision."

"And I guess if the chemo doesn't work, he is not responsible either," I joked.

That for me was the cherry on the top. I paused for a minute before walking out and looked around the adjacent room with the 12 armchairs and cancer patients. My heart sank when I looked at them going through the motions. Even though chemo was the promise of beating the dreaded disease, they all looked so ill, whether from the cancer or treatment or both. NONE of them looked better for it or like hope was on the horizon. I felt so sad for them and my overriding regret was that these people saw no way forward other than what was told to them. They were just succumbing due to a fear of, "What if I die because I don't do chemo."

I was done living my life in fear and thought, how disempowering… I can't become one of them – another statistic, with no guarantees, really... I'll take my chances and bear the consequences – the ones I can live with, rather than subject myself to someone else's decisions and I have to live the consequences of those, too. I can no longer live according so someone else's script.

I gladly signed the one-pager. As much as I respected that the doctors were offering what they believed was best protocol, I couldn't go against my gut again. I couldn't bear to succumb to fear again, as I had done many times in the past, and make the wrong decision for ME.

I couldn't help feeling compassion for the people who were paralysed by fear not only of the cancer but the thought that what if they didn't follow doctor's orders? While my heart was going out to these downhearted souls, I was feeling my own vulnerability. I wasn't out of the woods yet and I had my own work to do to heal my body fully – and I was doing it alone.

With that, I was out of there faster than I went in.

Next stop was radiation, which I consciously chose to do. I had done my research on the benefits and side effects, which made my decision easier and one with which I could comfortably live. I set my appointments daily for the required six weeks. I had my important WHY – to cauterise the affected area and to prevent anything untoward from progressing.

It was 10 December, a glorious midsummer's day when I started the treatments. The festive season was well underway but I was not feeling festive at all, just enormously grateful to be alive and in better spirits knowing the tumour was out.

The treatments drained my energy and I was often very

tired, so I didn't go anywhere or do anything much but stay at home, resting and sleeping. Sleep, of course, is the best way the body can restore and regenerate. This was a good and new thing for me. Billy and I would walk in the doggie park, visit our local coffee spot and watch life go by, and I welcomed visits from my very supportive friends. It was an undemanding period and the perfect time to read, reflect and immerse myself in the teachings and wisdom of the people who inspired me by healing themselves.

I was on a mission to get well and start my life afresh, this time in a different way, without seeking escape routes to distract me. I was not feeling particularly social – even though friends wanted to include me in their arrangements. I just needed to be with me and my loyal companion. My life has always been busy doing something, going somewhere, working, seeking, socialising and chasing. Now I was starting to see this quiet time as a gift – a chance to slow down and be.

I took time to further my well-being research around lifestyle and diets for people with cancer. I started to formulate my healing plan incorporating mind, body and spirit, realising they are all integrated parts of the whole that make up who we are. I started by revising my diet significantly and making conscious eating choices to eliminate acidic foods to ensure I kept my body alkaline.

A huge part of my illness, I realised, were toxins in the body, the result not just physically through food, impure water and air pollution but emotionally through negative thoughts and emotions. I discovered a well-renowned practice of coffee enemas to flush out the colon and rid the body of physical toxins, thereby lowering inflammation and increasing energy levels. It's hardly glamorous but I was on a mission to cleanse and heal myself from the inside out.

Meditation was an important daily ritual to quieten my monkey mind and focus on my future vision of myself and the future life I was creating. It set a positive tone for my day.

Exercise has always been an important part of my life for

my mind and my body. I needed to find a way to keep it up, even though I had very low energy. Vigorous exercise was not possible until a few weeks after my radiation. I needed time to recover from the draining effects of that, too. So I would take gentle walks with Billy and I did yoga three times a week to maintain my muscle strength.

I was loving the time to immerse myself in books and videos that inspired me and encouraged the changes I wanted to make. I found real-life examples of people who had gone through their own struggles in life – people who chose "the road less travelled" as their healing path and came out the other side the better for it. The common thread with all of my teachers was their knowing that healing the body was the result of healing the heart, and healing the heart was supported by changing the mind. They inspired my change and ignited the spark to start doing something about changing me, to change my life.

As I worked my way through these books and podcasts, it made me reflect on my life not as a victim but with understanding of the patterns in my life that had brought me to where I was, with two diagnoses of cancer. It was not my patterns alone but my repeating of certain patterns I had been observing through the generations – from my granny to my mother and now me, the perfect peacemakers and people-pleasers. Interestingly, when, as a young girl, I watched my mom and my gran, I was outraged at what they tolerated. When I asked why they did that, they both answered, "It's better to keep the peace for everyone's sake. You avoid arguments and conflict and then everybody is okay." NOT!

I didn't want to blame my history as I realised it would keep me a hostage to my past. I needed to find a way to do something about it and to do things differently to change the trajectory of my life. Not so easy!

The picture was clear of what I didn't want. I was fed up with being at the mercy of others' impositions, directions, instructions, bullying and fear-mongering to gain control of me, while inside me I was screaming "NO!"

I was exhausted from always shining and showing up to keep everyone happy or keep the peace – saying the right thing; going where I didn't really want to go; doing the things I didn't feel like doing and being who I wasn't. Worst of all, it wasn't working. I was miserable, not free to live my truth, and afraid to be me in case I was rejected or it would invite conflict.

I realised the Disease to Please was wreaking havoc with my mind and my heart. It controlled my decisions, putting pressure on me to perform and fulfil the should-do and must-do lists, to serve others' needs, rather than my own, with the hope it would yield love, approval or acceptance. I was always in conflict within myself between what I wanted and what was the "right thing to do" and the risk to me if I didn't comply.

Albert Einstein said: "Without changing our pattern of thought, we will not be able to solve the problems we created with our current patterns of thought." Change is never easy even if it is beneficial, which in most instances it is.

I journaled and summarised what I was learning from the sages I followed, so I could read and reinforce regularly what and how I needed to change. It was a way of thinking that was completely different from what I had known for 40 years.

To make changes:

- The right thing is most often not the easy thing to do and requires big kahunas to do so, because the risk of it being right for you is often not right for someone else, and can you live with those repercussions? (Einstein: "What is right is not always popular and what is popular is not always right.")
- We don't take action when life is going well – we need a shake up to wake up.
- Whether you make a change or speak your truth – you will be damned if you do and damned if you don't. There will be discomfort, disappointment or pain involved either way. It cannot be avoided. There is no way out – but through. Pain is something we humans will always unconsciously avoid whether

it is physical or emotional. What we don't realise is that what we are avoiding we are perpetuating because suppressed, unresolved or unexpressed emotion lands up in dis-ease and results ultimately in DISEASE!

The more I read, the more it was confirmed to me that the changes started with me. It also became clear to me that it would stir up discomfort not only in me but perhaps in those around me and it could be a lonely road. With that in mind, I became acutely aware that I would feel vulnerable during this phase. I needed to be mindful that, in my breaking away from old ways, those around me might get rattled because I was shifting away from the age-old dance to which we were accustomed. I understood that others' reactions might in some way resist my change, which could then trigger me back into my old patterns to keep the peace and hold relationships intact. I needed to be robust and unshakable in my stance or I was guaranteed of recycling my life. THAT was no longer an option.

An insight that I gained from the nightmare diagnosis, was how alone I felt. No one could walk my road for me, let alone make any of my final decisions. It was all up to me. This new journey of change would be no different because, as my homeopath told me: "Your road is your road we come into this world on our own and go out on our own." I was prepared and at peace with that because the alternative was, "resist and it will persist"

Of all the various teachers I respected and who inspired me, the one who spoke loudest to me was the late Dr Wayne Dyer. He changed his life at 60. So "it's never too late" was the message I got. He said, "If you change the way you look at things, the things you look at will change." His books inspired me because of his story. He walked his talk and was living proof of the wisdom and the insights he was sharing. It was clear to me that making physical changes to my lifestyle and diet was only a part of cleaning up my life. I needed to clear my thoughts, cleanse my heart and change the words I spoke. They were not serving me and my life.

It was a huge revelation when I realised how my thoughts, feelings, words and, of course, actions, had formed a part of how I arrived at this juncture in my life. A clear example of that was something I used to say to myself from 12 years old, "I never want to be a divorcee and I never want breast cancer."

Here I was with both. It was a bitter pill that I was a co-creator of my life's experiences. Now, how to change it all was a new venture into the unknown and it was going to be years of undoing and rebuilding. There was no way out, but through.

Taking a leap of faith into the unknown to explore and discover a new way of living was the only option for me. I was not going to repeat history. I am not in the recycling business where more pain is a guarantee. What I was convinced about was that by doing something different, I was equally guaranteed of something different even if I couldn't see it or didn't know what it would be. It would certainly be better than where I was currently, and that excited me.

As much as diet was one part of my plan, I also formulated my game plan for my inner well-being and explored various healing modalities. The first step came when I was introduced to a Reiki healer. I would see her once a week initially and she helped me clear the emotional and energy blockages stored in my cellular memory.

I also went regularly for reflexology to help me detox and restore balance on all levels. As the weeks went by I started to feel lighter and stronger. A sense of quiet began to settle inside me, the feeling of angst had subsided significantly and my heart felt more at ease. I think a contributing factor was that I had just finished my last radiation treatment and that chapter was now closed. The rest was up to me.

My life seemed to be turning the corner. My energy was improving, I was feeling better and my horizon looked clearer. Now that my body felt better, I was ready to tackle the emotional side and focus on creating a road map of the way I wanted to live in all areas of my life. I was ready to commit to myself the things that were important to me and the experiences I wanted to manifest, even if it meant I might be letting some things and some people go. It was time.

I crafted my vision board for a life I really wanted to live in a more focused and conscious way. I even reframed my wake-up call as a GIFT – a second chance, and I didn't want to squander it.

It had been five months since my operation, my radiation treatments were behind me and it was time for me to go for a check-up. My doctor wanted to see what the cancer markers were doing. Hopefully my choice of treatment and recovery plan had paid off. I was waiting in the reception of Dmitry's rooms. All I could hear was the tick of the clock and my heart beating. I was feeling nervous, with that all-too-familiar feeling of dread in my belly, reminiscent of my initial visit to him, when he had called me in to see my biopsy results.

He took the blood tests and neither of us wanted to wait three to five days for the outcome. He called for a "priority analysis" and said if I wanted to wait in the coffee shop till he received the report, he would call me when it was ready. It felt I was waiting for an eternity. I jumped at his call and sped upstairs. His big, warm smile said it all.

"Jo, you have the all clear. Bravo, whatever you did – bravo!"

This time the tears that streamed down my cheeks were tears of joy and gratitude. I hugged him amidst my thanks. Before I sped out of there to spread my good news, he said, "Jo, please just take care of yourself. I need to see you in six months. We can't just drop this as though it never happened. Precaution is important and we need to keep an eye on you. Just keep doing whatever you are doing, it seems to be working for you."

I don't know who was happier and more relieved, Dmitry or me. I turned to him and said, "Team effort, doc – thank you."

I couldn't wait to share my good news with my loving

and supportive friends and to thank them for holding my hand all the way through. It felt I had been given my ticket to freedom; a second chance at life but now in a different way.

THE DEMARTINI PLAN

Now I was ready for the next step on my odyssey. I wanted to craft a life that included a relationship. I had received a newsletter that Dr John Demartini was running a weekend seminar "Master Planning for your Life" and I signed up.

As intense as it was, it was also exciting. I had not thought about my life in such microscopic detail and it gave me something to look forward to AND commit to – like an adventure. I had an open road ahead of me of infinite possibility.

It was a new year and a new beginning and what better way to kick off the year than to create the master plan for my life? It held the promise of the start. Treatment was behind me and a blank canvas ahead of me – I was on a high.

I then embarked on my exciting journey with Dr Demartini and was ready for a fresh approach to life. One of the things in my master plan was to meet my life partner – I was ready to date again. I really wanted to get this one right and I had set out specific criteria for him and the kind of life I wanted.

The very next week I met a man, who would later be my husband. It all seemed surreal from where I had just come in the last few months. He pursued me with determination and consistent attention – enough to turn anyone's head and what most women would dream of. I couldn't believe how intently he cared about me. He went from someone who on the first date said he was never getting married, to someone who, three months later, proposed to me and asked me to move in with him. This blew me away that someone could love me that much so soon.

I thought, "Wow, can he be the one?"

However, if I was completely honest with myself then, there were visible signs from Day One that he wasn't. Yet I chose to minimise them because being in a relationship and having a sense of belonging with a family was important to me. I was falling back into my old pattern of just wanting to be loved and overriding the "no-go signs".

His whole family including his kids loved me and I felt that being part of this would be enough to make up for the rest … Growing old on my own was a very sad prospect. I often reflected during my cancer treatments how sad it was to be going through all of this alone with no one to turn to at the end of a tough day. I think now, in hindsight, that part of that vulnerability was still lingering in me.

It was six months into the relationship and I realised I made a mistake and the Disease to Please was back. I found myself compromising again and settling for what was not true for me. I wanted to be loved more than loving what I wanted. This, needless to say, resulted in me suppressing my thoughts and feelings and a growing unhappiness was developing. I felt stuck in something I didn't know how to get out of, short of just leaving, and even that was scary to unbundle. I needed an outlet and thought there must be a way to change my experience by changing the way I was doing things, because I was definitely repeating my past patterns. There was something that I needed to learn and do differently, so leaving was not an option right then.

I was referred to a personal transformation coach. My aim was to help myself understand why I kept finding myself in difficult relationships and perhaps also to gain a better understanding of the character I was living with. Perhaps this would help me to handle myself and situations with him better, which would ultimately benefit the relationship.

After one session I discovered this wasn't just any coach. He explained that the technique he used to enable change was NLP (neuro linguistic programming). I was fascinated. My eyes were being opened to a whole new level of understanding of human behaviour and what drives behaviour – including my own – and how to change it. This was also aligned to the work I was doing in my profession around behaviour change. It would add another dimension to it and enhance my offering, as I was experiencing it first-hand and could use this approach with my clients.

I came to understand that for change to happen and be sustainable, it was necessary to understand the patterns that were driving the behaviour before being able to reconstruct new patterns. I was suddenly realising that the choice of words we speak and thoughts we think, not only affects how we show up in the world but what shows up to meet us in our world. This was no quick fix but certainly worthwhile. I was fascinated by this because I could see how some of my patterns had got me into some less-than-satisfactory situations or relationships and I was determined to make my own improvements.

This experience opened my eyes to the world of neuroplasticity which offers hope that you are not confined to your patterns or your past. We can rewire our brains.

Dr Joe Dispenza says, "Thoughts that fire together wire together." So we can choose different thoughts and get different outcomes.

This was the start of an incredible journey of my own personal growth and some healing, too. I went in search of someone with whom I could study NLP , to change both my inner landscape and to be able to coach others who wanted to change theirs. My first step was to work on me before being able to help others.

As they say, "When the student is ready, the teacher appears." So I found Jevon in Hout Bay and this became my home of reflection and re-reviewing and relearning for the next two years. It took me on a rollercoaster ride of emotions as I worked through my old sabotaging patterns of behaviours. It was like a rebirth – painful and joyful! I discovered that my limiting beliefs of myself were the roadblock to the life I wanted deep down. I had to face my reality that I was co-creator of my painful relationships, and I got only what I allowed. That was a bitter pill to swallow.

Being a well-oiled peacemaker machine and completely conflict avoidant, I thought I was doing the right thing based on how I was raised – only to discover it was creating more pain than pleasure. I ran the spectrum of painful emotions from sadness to anger at myself that my life was a result of misguided choices and resentment at how I had sacrificed myself and who I am for nil return. And now I had to dig myself out of this hole. I knew it was going to be a lonely uphill battle and I was afraid. I knew I would need to face my adversaries and it would invite conflict, which terrified me, as it might cause the loss of these relationships.

I immersed myself in my studies with passion, commitment and determination because I understood the value of making these changes. Yet when I got back home, where I needed to integrate what I had learnt, I struggled.

Trying this new way made so much sense to me, yet each time I tried out my new tools and spoke my truth, I would hit a wall of either resistance or confrontation. This seemed futile and simply wasn't worth it – I just wanted peace.

My inner struggle was that as much as I believed in the skills I had learned, applying them wasn't easy because my environment was not supporting this new approach. I couldn't understand why this wasn't working ... It was like pushing water uphill. Ironically, when I returned to the original "formula": His tirade + I play nice + Keep the peace = Things go well ... there was relative harmony.

It was just all so hard to be true to me and apply my learning when I was constantly meeting a brick wall of resistance and conflict. The result was my resilience and resourcefulness were crumbling and I succumbed yet again to the line of least resistance that would keep the peace. I felt I was living my life as I did with my mother all over again – the characters were similar. Narcissists are scary to manage because you are always the problem.

I was so exhausted from always trying to be better and do more to fix our relationship. I kept on breaking my commitment to myself to do what was right for me and live my plan that I so carefully crafted during the Demartini workshop, only one year prior. In my quest for peace, I bypassed the fact that I was just recycling my old patterns and the patterns of my mother and grandmother, the ultimate peacekeepers. I was just co-creating more of what I didn't want and this was eroding me inside. I couldn't go on like this.

In spite of my personal circumstances, I had qualified as an NLP/HNLP practitioner, and it was a wonderful enhancement to my profession. I could add more value to my clients with more knowledge and better understanding of them and the situations they found themselves in. The results were evident and I found it hugely fulfilling and gratifying to witness the shifts in those with whom I worked.

Something that I recalled from my healing journey and was reinforced during my NLP training, was the fact that we are an integrated system of head (thoughts), heart (feelings), hand (body) and spirit. This was also reminiscent of the door opened to my awareness by Dr Northrup a few years before, that your body is the outer manifestation of your inner world.

I kept thinking, NLP works on one aspect of us: our thoughts, which fuels our feelings. However, I need to explore physical and spiritual healing avenues that would be complementary so I can serve my clients holistically.

Six months later, after doing some thinking and research, I finally decided on my next learning journey and enrolled in January 2012 to study therapeutic reflexology – a two-year international qualification. I had benefitted from it enormously while recovering from cancer. It helped with detoxing; de-stressing; improved circulation – there were numerous other benefits I enjoyed. I believed in it and wanted to add it to my service offering as a coach. I was excited, as I had a new-found passion and could immerse myself in something that was meaningful and had purpose.

I qualified two years later and, hot on the heels of that, I started my own practice at a Holistic Wellness Centre in

Bryanston. I was encouraged by my chiropractor to specialise in fertility as my core focus. Through my learnings from Dr Northrup's book, I had a great foundation in how our emotions and bodies were inextricably intertwined. This was definitely an area where I could add value to women's lives with whatever they were struggling with. Theirs was not just a physical condition, it had emotional roots and I was up for the challenge as I had walked that road myself. I found it hugely rewarding seeing the fruits of my efforts as I watched people's lives turn from hopeless to happiness. This helped to close the gap of self-worth, as I felt I was making a difference in at least one area of my life and what I was doing had a value that was appreciated.

All the while there was still another element missing for me though. It was the spiritual aspect of us that I felt also needed to be part of my holistic healing offering. I remembered the healing benefits from my Reiki treatments during my cancer journey. I felt that it would be beneficial and complementary to the NLP and reflexology and would complete the trilogy.

A year into my new practice, I entered my next phase of learning with a Reiki master. Two years later I completed and qualified as a Reiki master myself. This healing triad would be my unique offering as I believed in the power of these three modalities. This meant I could meet my clients where they were at and not be limited by one single therapy. Given that no two people are the same means that even if they have the same problem, it doesn't mean that they need or want the same solution. I now felt equipped and confident to go out and help my clients holistically and offer whichever point of departure that spoke to them. I wasn't a one-size-fits-all therapist. This excited me!

TAKING STOCK – IS IT WORKING?

It was 10 years since I was diagnosed with cancer; I was 53. A lot had changed. I was cancer free. I felt healthier and stronger than ever before. I was more confident in who I was. I had a thriving practice as a holistic healer and I was no longer a corporate facilitator. I was loving what I did and felt full at the end of every day. I also did my yoga teacher training certification and I never felt healthier than I was then. Yet I was still questioning myself if this was enough.

It was now time for my annual check-up with my gynae, which was always a stressful visit as I could never take for granted that all would be well, as much as I wanted to believe cancer was gone forever. Everything was fine, except my blood pressure was exceptionally low. So before I left his rooms he asked, "Are you okay, Jo, you are looking tired?"

The tears welled in my eyes. Was it that noticeable? The world outside was unaware because I showed up with a smile, ready to serve those in need. Yet inside I was screaming. I was in a marriage where I was dying inside. But how could I get out? I was embarrassed to be in another failed relationship and share the nightmare I was living. Being in the world of helping others and I couldn't help myself with all the knowledge I had; I was ashamed.

"Not really," I said quietly as the tears ran into my mouth. I briefly told him about my relationship and in his usual caring way he offered, "Jo, you can't do this to yourself – you have to look after your health and this is not good for you."

I knew what I needed to do. I just needed the strength and courage to do it... to get out.

The Disease to Please and suppressing my emotions and needs were making me sick. I wasn't sleeping at night, my stomach was always in a knot, my shoulders ached and my back muscles were tight from the "internal load I was carrying" and my joy was gone.

EXIT MY MOTHER – THE FINAL CURTAIN

During all this healing, I had made significant changes in my lifestyle and career, I had also married and my mother was back in my life. But let me explain to you about my mother through my eyes.

My mom was a full-time working mother; she ensured I was taken care of by my nanny Selina (who was probably more mother to me than my own mom. She knew me intimately and loved me equally as much). I went to the best school. I didn't struggle in the practical and material ways of life – it was just that my mother was never there, emotionally unavailable. She was busy in my step-father's business, running a home and entertaining guests. We also had my step-brother living with us. So our time was on Saturday mornings when we would run home errands and go grocery shopping together. I would go to the office with her in the school holidays unless I had been signed up for some extramural activities.

After university, and I started working at the age of 23, we had a sudden turn of events when my step-father skipped the country under a cloud. There was a warrant out for his arrest for fraud (which my mom and I discovered only after he left – he was allegedly going on another business trip). As a very young girl I had never liked him and as I grew older, I liked him less and less and trusted him even less. So this came as no surprise to me, not to mention his numerous affairs then uncovered to make matters worse. However, the devastating financial ramifications for my mother and me were traumatic. We had to sell our home and cars, give away two of our four dogs and be kindly supported by dear friends who supplemented my salary.

In 1988 we started finding our feet and thankfully we were also offered business opportunities through work associates and friends. Six months later, my mom and I united as a warrior tribe and started a business together.

We built synthetic athletic tracks and artificial turf (AstroTurf) hockey fields all over Southern Africa. It was quite an accomplishment in a male-dominated industry that was at the outset unfamiliar to us both. Construction is hard-core and very demanding and yet the accomplishment of the finished stadia was rewarding. I didn't have much of a life as I travelled extensively to project manage them and was home for probably three months a year.

The business became successful and a competitive force in the sporting arena. My mom became a significant player in the building industry and was appointed the first female president of the Master Builders' Association (MBSA) – an incredible achievement in a masculine industry. She was nicknamed Margaret Thatcher.

She became powerful in her own right and this spilled over into our business and our life. Her need to dominate everything and everyone, including me, was oppressive and I needed to get out before it destroyed our relationship. I craved the freedom to go and explore what else was out there. At 35 I was young enough and had the courage to make the change. After 12 years, I was losing myself in the stifling effects of my mother's control. I needed a life.

She was not happy yet she was accepting. She also made it very clear that once I left, there would be no turning back and no place for me there again. I agreed although it seemed rather harsh. I also left with the clothes on my back and no pay out – so I was starting from ground zero. It was scary yet ultimately empowering. My relationship with my mom had never been an easy one but I was always intent on "holding it together". So when I had left the business, her need to influence and at times control my decisions and choices, was still evident.

The final straw for me was five years later when it came to my 40th birthday. It was not only a milestone birthday but a defining moment and a crossroad where I had to face myself and my life and change tack. This meant testing our already fragile relationship.

She insisted on imposing her thoughts on my choice of celebration. That was when I knew I needed to draw a line in the sand and change the trajectory of my life. If I didn't stand my ground with her and speak my truth, this would be me for the rest of my life – conforming and pleasing my mother.

She had told me she wanted to give me a party at her house with her friends and mine, an event that she loved and I hated. It always ended the same way, with her drinking too much and becoming nasty and insulting. I did not want to be embarrassed in front of my boyfriend. I just didn't need or want a party – it's not how I wanted to celebrate my 40th birthday. I had been dating him quite seriously and would have much rather had a dinner with him and my mom, as they hadn't yet met.

When the time came for the final arrangements, my mother called me and said, "We need to talk about your birthday and the arrangements for the party." She still didn't listen to my wishes and I fell silent. I was feeling tense in my stomach knowing I needed to say what she would not want to hear. I finally responded, "Mom, you still haven't met Andreas and I would like you to meet him – that's more important to me than a party."

She indignantly retorted with: "Well, tell him to come to the party then …"

I was horrified and spun back with a sharp answer, "How can you expect him to come to a party and meet you for the first time and be flung into the lion's den among all your friends, knowing no one? That's stressful for me. It's neither a party nor fun."

"Well, what do you propose?" she seethed back.

I was shocked that a birthday celebration conversation could go so sour. I heaved a sigh in response, "Mom why can't we just keep this simple?"

She bit back: "You are the one making this difficult."

I was at a loss for words and frankly didn't want to carry on the conversation with the way it was going. So I arranged to see her on the Friday after work to talk about it.

I put the phone down fuming that something that should be happy for me was a battle because she wanted it her way AGAIN. I was frustrated with myself. I felt stifled. Being assertive with my mother always ended in conflict and tears. So I was avoiding it again. I ruminated in bed that night and my final thought was, Jo, is this how you are going to live the next 40 years of your life, chick? Allowing your mother to control your life because you fear the repercussions. You are a prisoner in your own life at 40. It ends now no matter what!

I hardly slept the next two nights and my stomach was in a knot. I knew this conversation was not going to end well. I woke up Friday morning with a sick feeling in my tummy and tried to muddle my way through the day at work, my thoughts consumed by the dreaded birthday discussion with my mother. I left work in a state of anxiety and just wished it was all over (whatever that meant). As I was driving to my mother's house, I just knew with crystal clarity that if I did not stand my ground with her today, this would be me for the rest of my life. THAT was not an option for me.

I arrived at her house and she was busy in the office, so I went through to the lounge and waited for her there. I felt as though I was being summoned to the headmistress's office. She walked in a little later with the all-too-familiar look of disapproval. God I hated that look.

"And so what have you decided?" she said sharply.

I could feel my hands shaking and sweating and my heart pounding when I responded tentatively, "I would Iike to go for dinner with you and Andreas so you can meet him. I really don't want a party and you don't need to go to all that effort and waste of money."

She looked at me with the stare that I always feared because I knew some kind of repercussion would follow.

"I have it all planned, so why can't you just bring him

along to the party and he can meet me then?"

"Mom, its awkward for me to bring him into a whole party of strangers and meet you for the first time. I'm uncomfortable with that."

"Surely he's a grown man and he can deal with it?"

She was determined to have her way and I knew it was time for me to step up and speak my truth regardless of the consequences. If I didn't, I would be hostage to my mother's control for the rest of my life.

"Mom, it doesn't feel right for me. I would rather he met you first, before meeting a whole bunch of strangers."

"So what are you saying, Joanne?"

Oh boy! That tone was the one I always dreaded. There was invariably a threat underlying it. Her eyes were cold and hard, her mouth was tight. Her perfectly coiffed chignon amplified the headmistress look. My body was shaking, and my stomach was in my throat. I could see which way this was going.

"Mom can't we just keep it simple and go out for a lovely meal together and you can meet Andreas? Perhaps we can also invite his mom because I spend a lot of time in her home?"

My mother's disdain was all over her face as she looked at me over her glasses with a look of deprecation.

"Oooooh, so now you are someone else's little darling? That arrangement doesn't suit me at all, so you can decide how this is going to go. Perhaps you would like to go and have your birthday with her then."

"Why does this have to be complicated, Mom?"

"The only one complicating things is you. So someone who has been in your life for eight months is more important than me who has been in your life for 40 years?"

"Mom how did you get to that? It's not true and you can't equate it that way." I could not fathom how she'd arrived at that twisted conclusion. I rolled my eyes in exasperation and I could no longer mask my frustration or bite my tongue. "Why do you have to turn this whole thing that should be a celebration into combat? It's my birthday after all. Shouldn't I be deciding how I want to celebrate it? Frankly with this kind of palaver I actually don't want to celebrate it at all."

"Joanne, you can do whatever you like but I am not interested in meeting his mother. It's enough that I have to meet him and we don't even know how long this relationship will last, given your history."

I looked at her in horror and disbelief that she could go so low with her scathing remarks.

My nausea was escalating into a cold sweat and I instantly retorted, "I have a better and much simpler idea and no one has to endure anything they don't want to. So why don't we just have breakfast, you and I? Then I will have dinner with Andreas and see his mom on the weekend. That way no one is put out or left out."

You could have cut the atmosphere with a knife. "Really?" she said with a wry look on her face. That one word felt like a loaded gun. It felt like a guillotine was about to drop above my head. The blood drained from my face and I wanted to run from the executioner, but I sat firm and still. "Is that your final decision, Joanne?" she uttered through gritted teeth and an icy stare.

I wanted to throw up I was so nauseous with fear. It felt as though she was throwing down the gauntlet. And this was my last chance to speak my truth irrespective of the consequences. I couldn't even look her directly in the eyes. It felt like the Titanic going down.

"Yes, it is, Mom." I felt the quiver in my voice.

"Well, you've made your final decision. Now get out of my house and don't darken my door again."

"But Mom that's …"

"You heard me Joanne – get out!"

I froze with shock at the finality of it all, even though a part of me was not surprised. The harsh reality that a mother could just cut you out over something like that horrified me. I had always known in my soul that I was on safe ground with my mother only while it was on her terms. I dared not buck the system.

I knew that I no longer wanted to live a life of threat and fear and it needed to end now before the second half of my life would die in the Disease to Please. The conversation was done and my life with my mom was over in one single sentence.

That was it. I didn't see my mother again until she walked into my ward prior to my cancer surgery.

That was then the start of a new chapter in my life. My mother returned – for who knew how long? It would be on her terms. We somehow bridged the gap although I felt it to be very tentative.

After my recovery, I was attending my Demartini Master Plan Workshop when I met my second husband. He and my mother seemed to hit it off, which made life easier even though they were seemingly very different. As time went on my mother became aware of the difficulties in my marriage and knew that most of them were driven by financial and business issues that my ex was navigating. Then one day my husband came home, "Jo, I have some news for you and you probably won't like it."

I stopped in my tracks and turned to look at him. "I am joining your mom in the business." My jaw dropped and my heart thumped so that I could feel it in my ears.

The news shocked and frightened me as I knew with every fibre of my being that this was the beginning of the end. I could almost see it. It had happened before. Another pattern. This time I just didn't know how it would end.

I said, "Both of you need to know one thing – I want no part of this. I am putting aside my prejudices and past and you can both do whatever you choose, just don't ever involve me in any way if and when it goes sideways. You both made the choice, you both bear the consequences. Just leave me out."

As if my marriage wasn't rocky enough, I now had my already shaky relationship with my mother being tested again.

I reminded my husband why I had left and that nothing has changed. "So I'm not sure how Maggie will be any different and why she will relinquish power to you. So manage your own expectations."

The months followed and, as predicted, the power struggles ensued, my husband came home enraged daily and it wasn't even six months later when it was all over. It took every ounce of my being to hold back from telling them, "I told you so."

The shock of all shocks was not that the two "wise ones" parted ways, but with that, my mother exited my life again. Without even a call or a conversation. I knew in my soul why. I had seen this movie before. In her mind, it was divided loyalty – a replay of the scenario that exploded around my 40th birthday. Yet somehow this time it didn't feel so bad.

At least I had to deal with only one of them now and I wasn't being pulled between my mother and husband and being forced to make a choice or decision. She tacitly made it easier for me and I never saw her again.

In spite of the fallout between mother and husband, I gained clarity and it was becoming clearer and "louder". He and my mother were the same type of character. Here again, like my two cancers: Who is the common factor? Joanne there is no coincidence – here is clearly another lesson to be learnt. You have more work to do – something more you need to face and change.

My relationship was on a rapid decline and gaining momentum. My husband and I were back in a financial squeeze and the arguments were rearing their ugly head and becoming more destructive. I would lend him money to keep the peace and if I questioned him or resisted in any way with valid reasons, a ruction would follow. The truth is I feared saying NO, even though it was eroding my savings and leaving myself with no safety net.

There was always a war inside me between: Don't be stupid, you will never see the money again. What are you doing to yourself? And: he is your husband; you need to support him without conditions. All I knew was I had to get out of this nightmare. I couldn't continue living this life. It was killing me.

What made matters worse, was the epiphany that came to me one morning early as I went to yoga. You have married your mother. They are two peas in a pod. They are both bullies, they control you through fear. Bullies have been your Achilles heel since school and a number of other occasions through your adult life. You have to end this cycle. If you don't stand up for yourself, break the shackles of your past and find your voice, you will keep repeating this pattern and your life will be a lifelong jail sentence. It will ultimately kill you one way or another.

It was like my a-ha day had been when I realised my role with both my cancer diagnoses. Once again, I was the common factor. And here I was again. The message was loud and clear: Joanne you have to get out of this mess and save your own life.

But "how and when" was the question. I was scared of the repercussions and the unknown and I was alone in my decision and the consequences.

Looking back on my life, I realised that my fear of rocking the boat by living my truth, fear of disapproval, losing love and not being accepted was my "hidden driver".

I recall a very "loud" and brutally honest message I received. It was from a very good man, one of my heartbreakers. He was a self-confessed, commitment-phobe and said to me one day, amidst my tears from his rejection: "You know, Jo, if you would be who you really are, you might get more of what you really want."

It was like a bucket of ice-cold water was hurled at me. But, man alive, it sobered me from the drunken stupor of my Disease to Please. It was a gift unbeknown to me then. I was looking for love in the wrong places, settling for less than I wanted and deserved, and choosing people who were not aligned with who I really was. I was ultimately not being true to myself. My life was a charade. I had to break free from my past and finally find myself, honour myself and fearlessly be myself.

The Disease to Please had ramped up to "fear if I don't

please". I feared that his rage would ultimately result in him kicking me out. Then what would happen to me? My savings were too depleted to put a roof over my dogs' heads and mine. It's a weird thing when you know what you doing is wrong and harmful to you, and yet the voice of fear threatens and paralyses you.

PART 3

Finally doing it right – divorce and Davidji

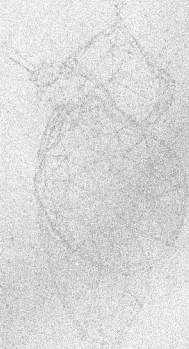

I knew what I had to do next. It was crystal clear.

While I was planning my exit, I continued my commitment to what I called Sacred Soul Sunday evenings when I would enjoy solace and sanctuary if only for a few hours a week. I would go to my meditation group at the Art of Living and share space and time with like-minded souls. It was my weekly spiritual top-up. This is where I had another light-bulb moment.

We had a discussion about growing pains and how the mind tricks us, with all the stories we sell ourselves, into avoiding the discomfort or pain that accompanies change and growth. My a-ha was, what we avoid, we perpetuate and pain is inevitable. There is no way out but through. As the adage goes "what you resist persists". In my case, staying was making me ill. As painful as it would be to leave many people I loved, it was going to be even worse to stay. So I would be damned if I did and damned if I didn't. I had to remind myself that fear has always held me hostage to my circumstances, whether it was my mother or my ex. My fear of repercussions was my ball and chain, be it conflict resulting in someone else's "displeasure", failure and losing face, or loss of love or a relationship.

The clear message was that staying in any toxic relationship guaranteed me a recycling of my past, which would become the best predictor of my future and I could not stomach another rodeo. The nett result would be living while I was dying inside. Therefore the risk in staying was higher than the risk of leaving. As Robin Sharma says, "Fear is just a lie you have rehearsed so many times you believe it's true."

I was digging deep to find the courage and strength to face the resistance to my leaving and the backlash that was unavoidable in all its forms. I had been through it with my mom and I was now being pushed to my edge again to take the leap of faith in spite of my fears. I knew deep down that making the change had to herald something different even if I had no idea how that would look; it had to be better than where I found myself. There was no way out but out. As Nelson Mandela said, "Courage is not the absence of fear – courage is moving beyond your fear because what's on the other side has a higher value."

From that day on my new mantra became: "Fear stagnation rather than risk regret".

And my journey to change began in earnest.

FANTASTIC FUNGI – PSILOCYBIN

Psilocybin is a celebrated vessel for expanding consciousness and healing the brain.

It is a tried and tested hallucinogenic and in some circles is more commonly known as magic mushrooms. Scientifically it transports you to an altered state of consciousness with many medical and psychological benefits. It also offers you a channel for mystical experiences. Psilocybin is judged by many, and frowned upon, as a recreational escape route from reality. You can view it in whichever way you choose.

Although I was free from the obvious shackles of my past patterns (my mother and my marriage), I knew I had a long road ahead to clear my mind, recalibrate my thoughts, align my head and my heart and rebuild the foundations of my life. My mind felt fragmented and scattered. It was like a juggler on steroids. Sleeping was not resting. I battled to sleep as my thoughts ran wild. When I did sleep, I would wake in the early hours relieved that I was in my own space with my dogs. I was out of that life physically and I could breathe. I had no one badgering me, no one to defend myself against.

I soaked up the peace in my environment, knowing that it was just me and my doggies. This was bliss. It was at night that my mind would pick up the pace and start recollecting past events. I would lie awake problem-solving, planning, carefully considering everything I needed to do, and the consequences. I just wanted this all behind me – to have peace in my heart; quiet in my mind and to live a simple life.

Equally important to me was my spirituality. It was my beacon of light and illuminated a horizon of hope. In some ways it was a private part of my life because I didn't want to defend what I believed in, and being open about it would just breed conflict. Journeying with Soma (magic mushrooms) was a part of my spirit life in which I had mystical experiences and gained many insights to life and my own life particularly.

Over the years I would visit a shaman in Cape Town on the pretext of work and would extend my stay so I could join her on her Soma retreats. Telling anybody that I was partaking in psilocybin would have raised eyebrows and questions. If my family knew, it would have caused an uproar and, with their limited knowledge of hallucinogenics/psychedelics, they would immediately have thought I was on a drug trip.

So in my new-found freedom and equal turmoil, one of the first things I did was connect with this shaman. I knew it would be medicine for my soul and this time I didn't need to go under cover. Coincidently this time she was hosting a retreat in Jo'burg. It all felt right and the timing was perfect.

It was a sunny afternoon in March as I was packing for my overnight stay with Monica, who was hosting the Soma journey. I was excited but a little nervous as you never knew how things would unfold. I had a baby sitter for Winston and Billy and I was ready to go on a journey within. I drove to the venue, an agricultural small holding north of Johannesburg. It was silent and peaceful, with a beautiful garden and giant trees that shaded the ceremony area. There I met my treasured bestie and soul sister Tracey, with two of her young adult children.

It was 6 p.m. The sun was just setting in a soft orange glow and the air was warm with a hint of a breeze. The birds were quietening, revealing just the gentle whisper of voices. The four of us found a space where we could camp under the stars, sheltered by the canopy of the trees. Although there were 20 other participants, we ensured we were not too close to the others. We laid out our cushions, pillows and blankets, had our full water bottles at our sides and sat quietly just BEING in the space. We watched others find their space and create their own cocoons for the night and contemplated what the night would bring. Each ceremony brings something different. It was not the first time for Tracey or me. Our fledglings had done magic mushrooms recreationally but not in ceremony and Tracey and

I knew they were in for an unforgettable ride for which they were not prepared.

It was 7 p.m. when the Mother of Mushrooms emerged, with her usual gracious presence and wisdom, from what we later discovered was the refreshment and bathroom area. She had five others at her side. She wore a long, simple soft dress with her traditional lightweight, purple poncho over her shoulders and flat, comfortable shoes. Her warm smile and gentle wise eyes were welcoming as she gave a loving look at each of us. Monica was about to prepare us all for the evening with an invocation and give us our dose of the medicinal fungus.

She appeared with grace and gentle energy, calm and kind. She warmly welcomed us all and proceeded to establish the ground rules and guidelines for the evening. She went on to introduce the five people at her side as the fire-keepers who were there to support us through the night in whichever way was needed. She oriented us to the facilities, like the bathrooms and the refreshment area, should we want something to eat or drink. She explained that once the effects of the journey wore off, there would be delicious soup and rolls available to nourish and ground us. She invited us to return thereafter to our spaces quietly and sleep till the morning when we could expect a hearty breakfast and enjoy a space with the other fellow travellers to share their experiences, ask questions and simply bask in whatever their journey had brought to them.

Finally, Monica explained the process. as a number of people were joining for the first time. She said, "I will come to you all and hand out your 'dose' together with a glass of honey and water mixture, for you to stir into your portion. Stir it well and then drink it all at once. Then you can enjoy the block of dark chocolate to sweeten the journey.

"Please be mindful that this is a sacred ceremony and to consider your fellow travellers. Each person's journey is personal, so please refrain from chatting to others or interfering in someone's process as it may take them away from their experience. The fire-keepers and I will take care of you all and keep the space safe."

Her final message was one of the most important of all: "Once you have received Soma please connect with her in quiet and stillness. Consider what your intention is for this ceremony and what answers you seek. This sets the tone for your journey. As she makes her way through your body, focus on your intention. I wish you all abundant blessings and a fruitful experience of healing and enlightenment."

Monica moved to a table set up with sacred Soma and we were called to receive our dose from her. With that we returned to our space, slowly consumed the mixture and allowed the experience to unfold. It is different for everyone and the effects were varied, but nothing harmful occurred. It is a pure form of hallucinogenic that has been beneficially used to reduce anxiety, alleviate PTSD, addiction, depression and more.

In a spiritual context, it dissolves for the duration of the journey (which can last up to six hours) the veils and layers that obscure our clarity of thought so that we can connect more lucidly with our higher consciousness. This was why I was there!

I was overwhelmed by what I had gone through over the years in my relationship and with my mother. The anxiety from my accumulated levels of stress had increased dramatically from the shock of the horrific events that unfolded over the years, until I was catapulted out. I needed clarity and guidance from spirit without the interference of the committee in my head.

As we sat quietly under the magnificent unpolluted night sky, my heart throbbed with apprehension as to what would be revealed to me. I started to feel the tingles in my body as the mushrooms took effect. I decided to lie down so my body could relax. I looked up at the moonlit sky and the galaxy of stars. I felt myself becoming lighter as I was being transported by the music to another level of consciousness, although I was fully aware of my surroundings. I knew my journey was beginning.

Initially I heard the gentle night sounds of frogs, crickets and owls. Then nature's music was interrupted by other sounds … other people's experiences. Some were laughing, others were crying, some were throwing up and others were vocal. Our little tribe was quiet and detached. Some fire-keepers sat through the night keeping vigil, others walked amongst us. All was taken care of and safe.

I felt myself slip into a vortex of sorts in the shape of a chakana, a stepped cross used by the Incas and known as an Andean cross. I started at one end and ultimately came out the opposite end. The journey through was excruciating. It felt as if I was in a washing machine being washed and rinsed at high speed. I was fully aware of where I was but the energy and physical discomfort of the experience was unbearably uncomfortable and I could not stop it. I just wanted to halt this merry-go-round by drinking water or coffee, eating something or walking about but I couldn't move. I couldn't have stood up if I tried.

I kept saying, "I want to stop this"; "Why does this have to be so hard?"; "Why do I do this to myself?"; "There must be an easier way"; "I can't do this anymore"; "I want to stop this"; "And this is going to continue for four to five hours". I was angry that I had put myself through this.

Then I would touch my heart space, breathe deeply and the feeling passed. The music changed to beautifully light and angelic notes and I felt relief, joy and gratitude for what I had come through, even though I couldn't fully identify it except for the physical part. I even found myself saying, "That was worth it – I am feeling blessed."

Then the music changed and I was back in the washing machine being washed and rinsed and washed and rinsed again. The same emotions came over me as before. I was resisting and battling to surrender to the experience. It seemed an eternity until I could place my hand on my heart, breathe through it and it would pass again. I would then be uplifted by the gentle angelic music and that feeling of relief that I was through it. I then felt enormous gratitude and that it had all been worthwhile.

This cycle repeated itself as I moved through different steps of the chakana. I could not articulate what it was that I was being washed and rinsed from, but my overall sense was an overriding feeling of gratitude.

There was a time in the middle of the chakana that I knew I was in another realm where I met Tracey and she had the same experience at more or less the halfway point in her journey. I knew this, not because I felt myself leave my body, but I felt it return, as it might after astral travelling. It was a place of sheer bliss and I was delighted to be hanging out there with my best friend. At some point I then returned to my body and continued in the washing machine. I was frustrated, seeing no end to this repeated cycle, until I remembered to place my hand on my heart and breathe through the discomfort in surrender.

Each time I went through this process it became easier and easier. The loud message for me was "what you resist persists – let go and release." And THAT was the "message in the mess". "Let it all go, all the old stuff, thought patterns and behaviours that don't serve you, fears, anxiety, trying to control an outcome to avoid conflict. The sooner you let it all go the freer you will be. What will be will be." So, "Let go and let God'" in Dr Wayne Dyer's words.

Finally I was out the other side. It felt like a lifetime that I had been on that journey and yet it probably was a lifetime of stuff to clear out. What was most profound for me was the feeling of lightness in my body, quiet in my heart and calm in my mind. I was basking in the afterglow of the journey and the enormous gratitude I felt for going through it all, no matter how tough it was.

I could hear the others in our posse stirring and suddenly I started to giggle. It persisted and progressed into secret laughing with some suppressed snorts as I didn't want to affect others and take them out of their experience. Tracey saw me and she began to bubble into unstoppable giggles. We ducked like naughty children under our blankets to avoid disturbing the others and reconnect with why we were there.

It was almost immediately after that when I received another message, not quite a voice or a visual sign, but it was a strong and undeniably clear communication – "laugh and play more".

I continued soaking up the energy of the journey and allowed the entrancing music to transport me to the beauty and love that was all around. It was a place where I could not only see but feel the interconnectedness of all things and beings. I was in awe of the true essence of what the Universe is all about. It is about us all being connected energetically in spite of our bloodlines. The essence of our being is love and harmony – no struggle, conflict or control of any kind – it is allowing and free flowing.

As I lay under the night sky illuminated by the moon, I understood that whatever we experience when we are back in our busy mind and lives, is confronted in our journeys, not necessarily directly and sometimes subtly. Our thoughts become clouded by the human-made world (that is, our daily experience); the busyness of life; the material world; the world of power, control; the varying forms of evolution to the good and not so good (whether it be science or technology.) It's all an illusion that drives our behaviour. This is why sometimes I have found myself in a conflict between what I want, feel and believe versus what is right and acceptable.

As I lay there quietly, I continued my reflections of what has always been true for me. Love has been my highest driver and value – it has been since I was a little girl. I believed in love stories and that love conquers all and everyone deserves to be loved unless they do unlovable things. At the heart of most people, there is goodness.

However, the world is one of competition, comparison and control and they drive people away from their true essence and start to alter who they are into what they think they are required to be if they are to be likeable, loveable and acceptable.

So journeying for me, in a sacred space with Soma, is like a coming home, where I can be fully me. It's a space where I can connect with my higher self, inner being and Source. I feel safe and open to receive the clarity that I seek, when my head is busy in day-to-day life.

It was just then that the next message came to me: "Your life is so much more than this bump in the road – focus on your life's work."

There were comfort and questions that came with this message. The comfort was that in the bigger scheme of my life, this nightmare would pass and clear the way for what is more important – my purpose. My question was "what is my purpose?" And then a very loud and powerful message followed: "Being invisible does not mean you are insignificant – your work is in the 'invisible realm' and that is your gift". Wow!

THAT was profound!

So many people personally and professionally have said to me, "Jo, you have touched thousands of lives just because of who you are. You allow people to feel seen, heard and understood – you just get it – no matter whom you encounter. You make us feel that who we are is what matters."

Others would say, "You tune into them and they feel safe to be themselves with you and, before they know it, you have unpacked their whole life in front of them and are helping them sift, sort and solve the issues they face. You are patient and kind and you listen to hear and understand – that's a gift."

A wonderful observation that I also hear and really means a lot to me is, "Jo you are so real, you unashamedly share your own raw truths and your humanness, which gives others permission and courage to share theirs."

So that evening was probably my most profound and crystal-clear journey yet. I believe it had to do with me being free to be me and not living a clandestine life.

I continued to savour the gentle free-flowing experience and felt open to receiving what I had longed to hear and see in their truest essence. I was in awe of the cosmos and the interconnectedness of everything as I gazed into the night sky. In the background I could faintly hear the widely varied music that would lift me into a state of bliss and lower me into reflectiveness. I could vaguely hear a wide range of emotions being expressed among the fellow travellers. Sprinkled in between was nature's music, birds and insects singing in their own harmony.

Then another message appeared: "You are about the truth." That was a loaded statement and had many elements to it. Yet I understood them all.

One of the promises I made to myself when I left my old life behind: "I will never tolerate lies and deception from anyone, no matter how small, because they cut the path for more, bigger dishonesty."

The biggest commitment I made to myself was: "I will never lie to myself again by accepting what is unacceptable, because that makes me a co-creator and therefore I am tacitly enabling continuation along that line."

I was starting to feel a gentle tiredness come over me as the effects of Soma were wearing off. I felt like I had run a marathon and was on a high from winning my own race. I felt an overriding sense of gratitude for the opportunity to be in a sacred space to heal and grow, created by my beloved elder, Monica, and to be held with love and care by her tribe members. I was equally grateful for this space to be connected to the cosmos and that I was able to hear the messages.

Of course, I would love to have known: "Okay, where to from here – the plan." Yet that's not how Spirit rolls, which was part of my learning – to tune in and listen and guidance will show up. I just have to remember to pause, clear my head and open my heart.

This journey also reinforced how important my spiritual path is as part of me being true to me.

As meditation guru Davidji would say: "What holds your Universe together and the stars apart?"

Some of the group were starting to come out of their experience and were in search of refreshments and nourishment. Tracey and I rose to get some of Monica's home-made soulful soup and freshly baked bread. It was so soothing and comforting after our cosmic ride and very grounding. In no time at all I found myself nestling into my sleeping bag under the stars and I dropped into a peaceful sleep with a full and grateful heart.

The next day we woke up with the sun rising and warming us and decided to go home rather than be involved in everybody's sharing of their varying experiences. Tracey and I just wanted to contain the experience in silent appreciation. We would speak about it together as the day unfolded. We quietly left after saying farewell and hugging our beloved sage with enormous gratitude for our night of gifts.

I went home energised and excited. I spent the afternoon researching truth and its depth of meaning, as I felt that although it was a fundamental principle of all our lives, it was not always easy to follow. The lessons were hard and fast.

I knew the key to speaking my truth was confidence in myself, having the courage to speak my truth in spite of the ramifications of loss and conflict. The most profound learning was that the greatest loss was the loss of myself in the heap of lies or excuses I was accepting, and the awareness that my excuses were a form of lies expressed through the ego. That also gets in the way of making the changes to live my life with more integrity to the commitments I make to myself. Self-integrity was my a-ha. I would not be swayed by ego to fit in with what others think or feel or say we should do. Ultimately living an authentic life is about being congruent with what I think, say and do. It seems so obvious, yet practically it was the truest test of honouring the self.

Part of my passion and purpose was: how could I encourage people with whom I work, who were navigating similar struggles, to share what is true for them without them feeling threatened and fearful in some way by the possible repercussions?

One way was to lead by example and share my own life experience, which holds credibility and demonstrates courage. Yet how could I make it compelling enough for them to speak their truth fearlessly, no matter the outcome.

In my research I found the secret to a sincere life of truth that I could hold myself accountable to, which held five levels of truth:

- Level 1: Telling the truth to yourself about yourself.
- Level 2: Telling the truth to yourself about another.
- Level 3: Telling the truth about yourself to another.
- Level 4: Telling the truth about another to that other.
- Level 5: Finally, telling the truth to everyone about everything.

The last one is the ultimate liberation, where the truth does set you free. It is just the how and the timing that need to be considered when delivering the message. However, this depends on the recipient and their frame of mind – it may not land as intended.

Dr Wayne Dyer says: "Speaking your truth is YOUR karma – what others do with it, is their karma."

That people may be unable to hear your truth is no reason not to speak it, otherwise you are tacitly making what is "not okay" to be "okay".

From that day forward I committed to consistently connect with Spirit as the source of my inner guidance. My journeys with Soma also became a constant ritual as part of honouring who I am and my truth and to continually gain the clarity that would lead me to a purpose-filled life.

I de-committed to the old excuse of "life gets in the way of prioritising the time to be still and go within". My meditation and yoga are rituals to keep me connected to me and would become important parts of my well-being and my life as a whole.

DIVING DEEP WITH DAVIDJI – MY CLEAN-UP CAMPAIGN

Part of my clean-up operation was not just leaving my relationship. That was just the key to unlocking the door behind which I had for so long been hostage inside my cave of fear. I needed to do some serious housekeeping by clearing cluttered thoughts and firing the unwelcome voices in my head which eroded my confidence and self-worth. I had to come clean with myself about what I had co-created by allowing the circumstances in which I found myself.

To do this I knew I needed to find stillness; to be quiet and on my own rather than busy myself with distractions and seeing friends. Of course, I was working and that occupied my time during the day in the weeks ahead. However, my evenings were quiet at home with my furry companions Billy and Winston. So I would take them for walks and then immerse myself in the enriching books that had been lying patiently on my bookshelves for years. I now had the time to read them so I could inspire my mind, feed my soul and be propelled forward towards the life I craved. My weekends were quiet with just the three of us and I would spend my time gardening, mosaicking or reading. I consciously chose this way of life, making only one social arrangement at weekends, which was mostly with my treasured Tracey.

I was committed to working in and on my inner garden. I was determined to weed out what was not serving me – the thoughts I was thinking and the feelings I was feeling, and to own the results of where these thoughts and feelings had led me. It was time to re-landscape my garden and plant new seeds that would grow into the life I truly wanted. It was time to reconnect with the teachers who fed my soul and from whom I could learn and grow from the inside out. Some of my inspirers were Dr Christiane Northrup; Dr Joe Dispenza; Dr Wayne Dyer; Esther Hicks; Louise Hay; and Deepak Chopra. The common thread with all of them is: "What you think, influences what you feel, which often determines your actions and who you become". My misaligned life is what led me to the mess from which I was digging myself out.

To start this inner journey required stillness, focus, commitment, discipline, alignment and self-integrity. Some years prior, I recalled a very close friend of mine in the US, Michele, who was also committed to her daily meditation. She introduced me to a fascinating man, Davidji, who is known in the mindfulness world as the velvet voice of meditation. She recommended his meditations to me one day while we were on a retreat in Bimini/Bahamas: "I know his meditation style will speak to you, so see where it takes you."

As I listened to his voice every morning with my fur babies next to me I drew a groundedness and strength from his messages and meditation. He was a man who made big changes in his life and was brutally honest about his journey. The more I practised his guided meditations daily, the more I was drawn to him.

Of all the gurus I followed, Davidji was the person who stood out strongest as the right teacher for me. His long white mane and bushy beard; his playful smile and quirky humour are his signature. His eagle eyes miss nothing – always observing, perceiving and seeing through the veils. His insights are sharp and clear and his wisdom is infinite. He is a humble man with an inner fire to share his passion. I had been following his meditations for a number of years, now I needed more and was ready to take the next step. I signed up for his Masters of Wisdom and Meditation teacher training.

Davidji helped me find the stillness within and guided me profoundly through my inner journey. I was drawn to him for a number of reasons – the unique and captivating way he shares his teachings, along with his experience and insights. The most compelling reason of all was his awe-inspiring story of personal transformation. He is not only an incredible teacher of meditation and other spiritual practices, but one of the finest examples of how you can change your life by changing your mind. He walks his talk.

Davidji made some radical changes and choices in his life. After a 20-year career in the financial sector of mergers and acquisitions in Wall Street, he made a life-changing decision to quit that world. It was instigated by one of his unsuspecting "teachers", an old beggar who caught him unawares one day as he was returning to his office from a meeting. This vagrant tried a number of times to attract Davidji's attention and after a few attempts, Davidji, deep in thought, stopped and turned to the dishevelled man in annoyance. The man looked up at him and said, "And what do you think they will write on your gravestone one day?"

This rattled Davidji. He decided to not go back to the office and went home. He shared his experience and resultant inner turmoil with his wife. It was his tipping point for change in the way he was living his life. That's where his journey to "wholeness" began. He went on his own journey of self-discovery starting with Deepak Chopra, which culminated in him joining the Chopra Foundation as COO, working with Deepak and Dr David Simon (his mentor and friend) for a decade. He became their lead educator and then the first dean of the Chopra Centre, where he trained more than 300,000 people to meditate and certified more than 2500 meditation teachers. He has since moved on to continue his teaching independently after his dear friend and mentor passed away.

He continues to help thousands of people change their lives by transforming themselves using mindfulness, meditation and stress release. He shares mystical and ancient wisdom from Eastern philosophies and age-old traditions, and from his own learnings and experiences. He teaches and practises what he teaches, which for me, sets him apart and makes him heartfelt, authentic and certainly a role model to me and many thousands of people around the world.

As the traditional saying goes: "When the student is ready the teacher appears" (Tao Te Ching).

It was an autumn Sunday afternoon in May 2016. I received one of Davidji's newsletters. He was offering a six-month meditation teacher training certification starting in August – my birthday month. It would initially be online and would culminate with an in-residence immersion for a week, in Carlsbad, San Diego, California.

Perfect timing! I thought.

It was such a strong feeling that drew me to this programme that even the cost of it didn't sway me. I knew I needed to do this for me and I would find a way to pay for it. Not doing it was not an option. I wanted to move forward in my life, deeply rooted to myself and what is true for me. Davidji was offering all the touch points that I believed I needed and wanted to keep me anchored to my true north, so I could live my truest life fearlessly, as unshakable me.

I always aspired to walking my talk and yet somehow often found myself compromising what was true for me, to please someone else's agenda, which always left me internally conflicted, restless and never at peace. No wonder I wasn't confident to be me, because my self-worth was derived from others' approval.

After my last relationship, I had to ask myself three harsh questions:

- When would it be enough sacrificing of my happiness for someone else's?
- When would I stop trading authenticity for approval?
- Was I going to live the second half of my life the same way I lived the first?

I was done with reading inspiring books, admiring their authors and aligning myself with them, yet I hadn't put the teachings into practice. Living the spiritual life vicariously through the teachers that wrote these books and sharing their wisdom was one thing, but I hadn't embodied the lessons and was certainly not living them.

I felt a fraud reading incredible books and learning about these life principles and philosophies and talking about them with conviction, when actually my life was anything but that. It was a heap of contradictions. Especially in my profession, congruence is very important to me and it has now become a personal value to hold myself accountable when I make choices.

"It's enough Joanne – stop reading about it and admiring it, start living it."

It was time to leave the spectator seats and climb into the ring. So I embarked on a journey with Davidji, which was an adventure of itself. It was a combination of ancient philosophies and principles, with deep reflection, practical application and integration. There were no get-out-of-jail passes to just read, learn, listen, discuss and move on. Ooooooooooh nooooo sireeee …

It was a wonder-filled and eye-opening journey yet, at the same time, tough, because learning something is one thing, but honouring it by applying it is when the rubber hits the road. The reality was: to change my life I had to face my life. It was a bitter-sweet experience, incredible and rewarding but also an emotional boot camp.

The biggest "come to Jesus" moment was when I had to face the fire of my own reality in my final assignment, before attending the in-residence immersion. Davidji asked us: "What is your winning formula that you have created, that you think makes you loveable or likeable?"

I didn't have to think about it too long, as it was like an old familiar friend I had known for years and who visited me often. It had become a self-sabotaging habit. It turned out to not be my friend at all. The life that brought me to this point flashed through my mind like a horror movie.

Growing up as an only child with working parents, I lived in my own world of daydreams, hopes, wishes and fairy tales. Everything lead to a "happily ever after". My mom was quite the opposite – the realist and pragmatist. I was okay with her being who she was, but my frustration from an early age was that she seemed not okay with me being me. I was always being corrected, criticised or chastised about something. "You are too sensitive; you are too emotional; you are too transparent; you are like an open book; you are setting yourself up to be used and abused; stop thinking everyone is nice and good, you will always be disappointed; you give too much of your heart away. It will never be appreciated. People will take advantage of you."

My inner turmoil with: "am I doing what's right?"; "am I acceptable?"; "do they approve?"; "I don't fit in or belong" was my struggle. My mother always had something negative to say about the friends I had. At school it was always "you don't work or try hard enough". If I was in the B team then "why aren't you in the A team?" If I got 80%, which was rare, then "where is the other 20%; you are just being lazy". This criticism accompanied me throughout my life in all I did, including the choices I made. If it wasn't on her approval list, it was out. And here is where the roots of my Disease to Please were formed.

I knew nothing about self-worth or self-esteem, what that meant or how it was developed. All I knew was that I never felt confident about myself in any way. My decisions were based on fear of any repercussions if I displeased my main anchor, my mother. What would happen to me? And that frightened me. I didn't have any real friends. I hung out with people so as not to be alone at school, as I didn't really fit in for many reasons. My mom and step-dad were very strict. I wasn't allowed to go to the events to which others were permitted. I never challenged the status quo, as that would elicit drama at home. I was a big avoider of conflict. There was already enough of that between my parents. My pets were my constant companions, my granny and my nanny were my sources of refuge. I was terribly self-conscious because I was plain. Some kids at school would tease me as "fat Forbes".

When I went with my parents to visit their friends, they wanted me to just "go and make friends" with the other kids. I hated it. I felt awkward and uncomfortable. I would have preferred just to sit quietly with the adults or be at home with my dogs. I wasn't outgoing and I never felt confident hanging out with other kids. I didn't know how to be my own person. All I was taught was how to occupy myself, amuse myself and not expect others to be my entertainment. For starters, I went to a convent where girls can be pretty nasty and there was no exposure to boys. I didn't grow up with brothers so I wasn't equipped or confident around boys. With all these inner struggles and inner dialogues, I found myself often feeling very sad and crying silently with my dogs: "I don't belong in this world". All the while I questioned life: "There must be a better place than this. It shouldn't be such a sad place."

So the only way of keeping my hopes alive was by escaping into my daydreams and acting out my dreams more and more.

My mom would often say, "You are very quiet, what are you up to?"

My standard answer would be, "I'm just playing."

Even though she thought I was just entertaining myself with my Barbie doll and my dogs, I was quite serious about my daydreams. They were the secret reality I seeking. I held onto dreams of finding my hero and marrying him and living happily ever after. These dreams were my happy place. I would watch love-story movies and read love-story books and fantasise about that happening to me. As I grew older, this fantasy seemed to elude me. At school and at university everyone else seemed to have boyfriends. It seemed easy and natural for them and left me feeling there was something wrong with me. This reinforced my sadness and, more so, my worthlessness that no one was interested in me and I wasn't interesting or good enough.

If I shared this with my mother, she would say to me, "Laugh and the world laughs with you – cry and you cry alone." That was a very sad concept for me and meant that I had just to show up with a smile regardless of what was going on in my world. No one would be interested. "So how would I make myself a person people would like?"

As I grew into my twenties and started working, I was naturally exposed to a wider circle of people and was starting to meet men. Of course, my frame of reference regarding men was fractured because my dad moved on with his life when I was 18 months and my step-father was a bully and physically abusive. So to be admired and attractive – I guess like birds do – I fluffed my feathers and flirted. I was colourful, witty, playful and bright. People seemingly responded to this "butterfly" as I was once called.

However, as much as I was attracting men into my life, they were neither relationship material, nor the kind I was really looking for, and were certainly not good for me. After two to three months they would vanish. I couldn't understand why or what I had done. This really eroded my self-worth and self-esteem. So I would keep trying harder and do more and be more. This was all I knew. Yet that wasn't winning the prize. I didn't know how to break this painful cycle until I met Raymond. He was a really great guy, a good and kind person. Yet when it came to commitment, the relationship started to evaporate as all the others had done, and this was yet another painful disappointment.

"You are such a nice girl – you are too good for me – you are marriage material and I can't give you that."

I broke down into tears of despair. "Why does this keep happening to me?" I choked.

Raymond admitted that he was commitment phobic based on his own history. I was inconsolable. He was quite taken aback by my tears and somewhat helpless in his attempt to comfort me. Then amidst my flood of tears, like a bucket of ice-cold water in my face, he shocked me with an unexpected and sobering response, "Jo, you show up as this together, sorted, grounded, confident, independent and self-sufficient woman who doesn't need anyone … I had no idea you could be so hurt and affected." He paused with concern before continuing, "And perhaps if you would be more of who you truly are, you might attract more of what you truly want." Ouch! That hurt too. Yet I could hear the ring of truth to it and it was a bitter pill to swallow. In the end, it was a gift – the gift of truth.

And that was my "winning formula" – shining up bouncy, bright and breezy and being whatever I needed to be to get the love I desired. After a few weeks or a couple of months, this formula was then predictably followed by the heartache of love continually eluding me.

This sad cycle kept repeating itself like a stuck record throughout my young life and here I was halfway through my life at 51. Now how was I going to change it? I felt frustrated and despondent – I couldn't go on like this for the next half of my life. All I so desperately wanted was to be loved and I didn't know why it was it so hard.

And now, after all these years, like a lightning bolt, I was struck by my reality in my assignment. After submitting this assignment with a measure of shame attached to it, I felt quite sad to realise that all these years I had been like an actress, showing up in this role so I could be part of a show and popular with my audience... and all the while knowing it wasn't who I really was.

As if that wasn't enough, the ultimate bomb dropped when we submitted this assignment to Davidji and he responded with: "THAT is only PART 1! We are not done. Part 2 is: at what cost?"

It was like Davidji had pulled the pin on a hand grenade and it had exploded in my face. I had to confront what I had done to myself; what I had allowed and co-created that took me to the lowest ebb of where I was, in my relationship choices. It had cost me my self-worth, self-confidence and self-esteem.

I had to face the fact that I was reliant on others making me feel good, worthy, valued, appreciated and loved. What I later learned, in fact, was that the irony of it all is that self-worth, self-confidence and self-esteem come from the self.

I suddenly realised how much energy I had expended trying to be this person so I would be accepted, loved and belong, and then the realisation that in seeking acceptance and approval outside of myself, was exhausting and unfulfilling because I wasn't being me and indirectly I wasn't accepting me. I didn't see me as good enough, yet I was hoping others would. I cried for days thinking where do I begin to climb out of this hole I had dug for myself? There was no one to blame, nowhere to hide or no way to escape this realisation. No one could help me out, except me. I got me in and I had to get me out.

It felt like I was facing Mount Everest. It was scary, lonely, and heavy and felt insurmountable. Where would I begin and how would I get to the light side or 'bright' side? Interestingly I also became angry with Davidji and the process, because I had gone to hell and back and this felt like I was there again, digging myself out.

He quoted the Upanishads (Vedic book of Hindu philosophy): "You are what your deepest desire is. As is your desire, so is your intention. As is your intention so is your will. As is your will, so is your deed. As is your deed, so is your destiny".

This was a huge light-bulb moment that life wasn't happening to me. Life was happening because of me. I was hit by a flood of emotions ranging from anger at myself for how I had sold myself down the river, to resentment for the time I had wasted on futile pursuits of love and happiness, followed by a deep sadness that I had wasted my heart in vain on worthless relationships. Here I was, having to pick up the pieces of my heart and rewire my mind to heal my heart and start afresh, in a new way, with clarity and confidence.

My realisation was that change could really happen only when the pain of where I was exceeded the pain of changing.

This experience was ultimately the best thing that could ever have happened to me and I will be forever grateful to Davidji for the tough love.

It was one of the most empowering and enriching chapters of my life because, for the first time, I actually took the reins of my own life, jumped into the saddle without riding lessons, and was willing to learn, if it would take me to a better place.

So my next step was: "F*ck it – Just do it!" as per Richard Branson's book. And I didn't look back.

PART 4

The adventure begins – onwards and upwards

Part of recreating my life was not only through finding the teachers who could help me and inspire me to grow as a person, exploring life more and discovering more of who I really am and want to be.

An important part of this self-discovery journey for me was challenging myself in unchartered territory and exploring my life through travel. Elizabeth Gilbert's book Eat Pray Love really reminded me of my love for adventure and inspired this next chapter of my life. I had been to Italy, which was both beautiful and painful. I had been to Bali, which was also beautiful and painful. Both trips had been with my ex. Now I was taking my own journey, alone, to somewhere new and completely different, that spoke to my soul. It was the continuation of my journey with Davidji, which was emotional and spiritual, and where I had built a strong foundation on which to build my truest and strongest life. I wanted to anchor into some of the ancient philosophies, spiritual wisdom and traditions I studied from old and modern masters. I wanted to meet them at their source – to connect with them in my soul and integrate it all fully so it became a way of life. So I took off to India for a month with an itinerary of specific places I wanted to visit on my odyssey. Other than that, I had no plans. My aim was to just explore myself and life through all my senses in a soulful place, release the old me, heal me and come back home with clarity and peace in my heart.

INDIA – MY LIBERATION

My personal pilgrimage to India was a gift to me. It was not a holiday I sought – it was a catalyst for change that I needed, in whatever way it presented itself. Not even the naysayers threw me off. They said, "What's wrong with you, a blonde woman going to India on her own?"; "You are taking such a risk going to that country – you could get sick from the food and the filth"; "Is it safe for you to go alone?"; and "It's so filthy, and all the poverty – you will be swamped and hustled by people".

I was long past the phase in my life during which I was going to do what people approved of and I was not waiting for anybody to accompany me to do the things I wanted to do. If I had to wait for the person or the right time, I might never get to do the things for which my heart yearned. The only thing I would get sick from is the Disease to Please. Nothing was going to stop me. This was something I really wanted and needed to do on my own. It was that important to me and for me.

I remembered from watching Eat Pray Love and listening to people who had been to India say it had reshaped their lives in some way, and in different ways. I would welcome whatever that would be, for me to live the life I was creating – simple, peaceful and enriching. It was time to unplug from my world as I knew it and travel with a blank, in spite of the naysayers. I had an inner drive that surpassed any logic – it was a feeling deep in my belly and nothing was going to stop me – not even fear. I was filled with excitement, anticipation, curiosity, wonder and proud of myself for doing this – for me!

It was early summer in October of 2016 and Justin Bieber's song Love Yourself was topping the charts when I started my journey to India. The lyrics were almost prophetic, as I sat at OR Tambo International Airport in Johannesburg, waiting to board my flight and imagining what lay ahead. I promised myself three things. I would:

1. Take things at a gentle pace so I could absorb the experience;
2. Feel more and think less – some things are meant to be felt and not analysed; and
3. Do fewer things deeply than more things superficially.

As I landed in India, the dawn was breaking in a golden light. The air was balmy as I walked out of the airport. My journey from the airport to my hermitage was not only an eye-opener on so many levels, it was also a real feast for all the senses. The sheer numbers of people in any given space made up an endless sea of faces. The cacophony of sounds, although out of tune, were somehow in harmony with the environment. The composition of varied fragrances was fascinating to deconstruct. The brilliant, beautiful colours were like an arrangement of rainbows. My senses were ignited, my soul was singing, my heart was dancing – this was the start of an incredible journey.

I had only a month in India and I planned to visit specific places, each for its own reasons. So I started with the popular tourist part of the itinerary, the Golden Triangle – Delhi, Agra and Jaipur – to visit the famous sights that made up part of India's history. I progressed for the second half of my trip to Varanasi and Rishikesh for the more spiritual locations. I guess it was the yin and the yang of my trip – the tourist sites versus the spiritual places.

My first day was full, as I visited significant places of interest. I was giddy with excitement now finally to be in the country I had longed to visit. Of course, India also has strong ties with South Africa politically and commercially but for me it was the spiritual element that was most meaningful. I started by visiting the ancient Jama Masjid (mosque). It was enormous in structure, powerful in its presence, intricate in architecture, and thronging with tourists and devotees. It was a lot to digest.

Not far from the masjid, I entered the biggest market

in Delhi, Chandni Chowk. It was jaw-droppingly huge –
the sheer vastness of it and the crowds of people were hard
to comprehend. The little streets that separated the various
sections were lined by electricity poles connected by spaghetti
wiring. The market was permeated by an array of aromas
of cooked foods, spices, incense, masala chai, camphor, fruit
and vegetables. It was jam packed and abuzz with traders,
shoppers, tourists, beggars, dogs, cows, tuk-tuks and donkey
carts. Buses, vans and cars were permitted only in areas where
there was space to move them. What blew my mind was the
gentle, steady movement. Nobody was impatient, there was
no road rage or abuse. I felt there was a sense acceptance of
what is and allowing it all to happen in its own time. It was
organised chaos at its best and it was amazing to witness.
Incredible India!

In contrast Mahatma Gandhi's resting place, Raj Ghat,
was completely tranquil. Although there were hundreds of
visitors, there was respect in the way they moved around
his tombstone. There was gentleness in the way they walked
through the Gandhi Memorial Museum to see pictures, books
and memorabilia that were part of Gandhi's life. Exhibits
included personal items, such as his dhoti, shawl, walking
sticks and glasses – even one of the bullets that took his life.
It was deeply emotional for me. I couldn't stop the stream of
mystical tears that flowed down my cheeks.

This man stood for so much and asked for so little. He
wanted respect for humanity no matter what their social
standing. He believed that to know and serve the people as
they needed to be served, he needed to live among them. His
humility, humanity and integrity were worthy causes and still
palpable. He saw service not as a sacrifice – he knew it to be his
calling. A quiet, unassuming, small man but a giant in spirit.

I felt so full and exhilarated from such an enriching day.
It was only Day One and yet I was emotionally exhausted. I
needed to digest and process it all. I ensured I honoured my
commitment at Jo'burg airport not to let the 32 days go by in a

blur and so defeat my objective in India.

What did this all mean to me in my life back home in SA? So I pondered about how to enjoy a gentle evening with a light simple meal. Somewhere relatively lowkey. I decided to sample, at Janpath market, the simple street food that came highly recommended by my guide. It was not as frenetic as Chandni Chowk. It was a lot smaller and more Tibetan in its offerings. It was the perfect place for me to just sit and be. I ambled past the stalls, chatted to some local traders (I was interested in buying some kurtas and scarfs) and sampled the delicacies from the food market. I felt exhilarated being anonymous as I percolated my experiences of the day. That was my kind of freedom.

In the days that followed, I went to see the significant Taj Mahal in Agra. The story behind it being built was beautiful and the handwork to build it over 17 years, was astounding. I moved on to Jaipur, the capital of Rajasthan state, and was glad I had seen it. The palaces were architectural masterpieces, and their history intriguing, yet my heart couldn't connect with them. What fascinated me was the Jantar Mantar – the world's largest stone sundial that was hand built and is still used today. It amazed me how this phenomenal instrument can so accurately predict the time and movement of celestial bodies like the sun and moon. It blew my mind.

The next stage of my journey was to one of the oldest cities in the world and spiritual capital of India, Varanasi. It's the city that draws Hindu pilgrims who bathe in the Ganges River's sacred waters and where celebrations of life and death are held. (This river is revered locally as Mother Ganga.)

At the time that I was there, Muslims, Hindus and Sikhs alike were celebrating Diwali, the festival of lights. The narrow, winding streets were overflowing with pilgrims and visitors flocking to Mother Ganga. All the shops were interspersed with vibrant splashes of marigolds that they were making into necklaces and other arrangements to sell for Diwali. This flower is significant because it represents the sun, symbolizing brightness and positive energy and it is used for a variety of festivities.

Varanasi was buzzing and busy yet there was a gentleness about it – nothing frenetic or agitated. There were no road signs, street names for directions; no traffic lights, traffic circles or traffic police to move people and vehicles in some sort of order. It all just happened in its own rhythm without casualties. I was in awe.

My walk down to Mother Ganga at 3.30 a.m. to experience life on the river was an eye- opener and touched my soul on a deep level. Hundreds of people flocked towards the grand spiritual river to cleanse their souls, do their washing, carry out their morning rituals and ablutions and perform the last rites of the lives that had passed. It was an interesting mixture of activities and their respective emotions. The most fascinating for me was the river itself – gentle and majestic and at the same time brown and polluted. She flowed gently along carrying boats and leaves. People were swimming and washing. A dead cow floated by. Life was happening.

While the day was well underway for many people, the warm glow of the dawn was unfolding slowly on the horizon. A bright ball of red was surfacing as a message of hope for the new day. The sun was rich, bold and beautiful as it rose into the sky, perfectly and quietly. It was the complete opposite of what many could have perceived as filth: the noise of people worshipping, crying and talking; of motorists hooting; and the putrid smells of burning pyres; squalor and incense. Yet for me, it was real life, raw and true as life happens. It isn't always pretty. It's sweet and sour and I was in my element.

This is what travel means to me, witnessing life and learning from other cultures. Seeing how it shapes, influences or affects my life. I took my time to notice the details of my environment and appreciate the privilege of the experience.

I continued my day gently walking along the ghats beside the holiest river in the country.

Most of the ghats, riverfront steps leading to the banks

of the river, are where bathing and puja ceremonies (acts of worship) take place, though two are used exclusively as cremation sites. I participated in a Hindu ritual, called the Aarti Ceremony, held every sunset. The ceremony uses fire as an offering to the Maa Ganga, goddess of the river to clear and release all hindrances. I watched as lamps were lit and encircled by pandits (Hindu priests), accompanied by lively dance and songs of devotion.

As I sat watching devotees arrive for their daily ritual, two street dogs affectionately curled up at my feet. I had lost my precious Billy to cancer five months prior and I felt comforted by these local fur babies.

The ritual included an assortment of people from all walks of life, each coming for their own reasons. There was no exclusivity – everyone was welcome – including goats and street dogs. Even though I was an outsider, I felt welcome and included, as the ladies who sat beside me connected with me in total fascination and curiosity. What was a white Western middle-aged woman doing here on her own? There was no judgement, just total acceptance. Language was not a barrier, they even invited me to take my own offering during the ceremony (a collection of items that represent the five elements) and showed me how to perform the prayer ritual and place my offering on the river at the appropriate time as a blessing. There were no words exchanged, just hand gestures and smiles of warmth and total acceptance. That truly touched my heart – how simply and beautifully connections can be made without words.

Again my day ended with my heart overflowing with the enormity of what I had witnessed and shared. After the sacred ceremony, I had a light meal at the haveli, a traditional townhouse where I was staying, and turned in for the night feeling full in my heart, enriched, moved and a very happy tired.

My next destination, the holy city of Rishikesh, was the yoga and meditation capital of the world. This is where I wanted to be more than just an observer – I wanted to be a participant of this reality. I arranged to stay for part of my time in Rishikesh in the Parmarth Niketan Ashram. It's the main one and its location was perfect. I could walk everywhere.

It is a true spiritual haven alongside the Holy Mother Ganga in the foothills of the Himalayas. Anyone is welcome. There is no discrimination of race, gender, nationality, religion, caste or creed. This would my home for a week, where I could immerse myself in a life of "seva" – the Sanskrit word for service. It involved physical work and practical tasks to demonstrate selfless service in the form of cooking, cleaning, serving meals or gardening, and included devotional prayer or meditation as part of the daily rituals. Here, too, the Aarti ceremony was performed at sunset on the river banks. It would be time of reflection for me at the close of each day, and of silent prayer in gratitude for the time and opportunity to have this experience.

Living life in an ashram was a humbling experience – basics and the little things we take for granted were brought to reality: like the journey our food takes from seeds, to cultivation, harvesting, conversion to food and presentation. My gratitude was for the reminder of how simple life can be, with so much richness and fulfilment, and the feeling of time slowing down because we were living with more consciousness and were ever present in everything we did. There were no urgent demands, no rushing from here to there and no trying to do as much apossible in a day. Our practice of mindfulness was enriched by being disallowed use of our electronic devices, so we were free from distraction from the world outside. This was true liberation. We were even encouraged at certain times of the day to observe noble silence. It made me aware of engaging in conscious conversation that was meaningful or necessary when we did speak. All we had was the here and now – moment by moment being fully present in whatever activity we were managing and with our thoughts and feelings. It was so freeing knowing there were no pressures, demands or urgency other than your allocated tasks at the scheduled time on the roster. It was humbling to be part of gathering our food in the gardens to prepare our meals and to serve the meal to others as an act of conscious service. My overriding sense of inner peace left my heart feeling open and my mind unfettered. The gift was a real sense of community among total strangers from all over the world just coming together in search of tranquillity and harmony.

After I left the ashram, I stayed on for another four days so I could experience the rest of Rishikesh as a visitor and explore the holy city. I visited the Beatles' ashram where this iconic band had composed some of their best songs and were at their most productive as songwriters.

I was almost at the end of my journey, the day after I left the ashram, when I decided I would scatter Billy's ashes on the sacred river and then go for a blessing at the temple after the Aarti ceremony. It was the perfect way and place to honour my best friend.

Mother Ganga became a real source of comfort to me as I worked through some tough emotions of love and loss over the time I was in India. This was a particularly glorious and sunny day, with featherlike clouds scattered across the bright blue sky. I decided to do my meditation at the river's edge and took the box of Billy's ashes with me. I wanted to honour his life in a special place. When I knew I was going to India, I had decided then I would find the right place to set Billy's ashes free.

I sat beside the river. The sunlight was glistening on the soothing turquoise water as it moved gently downstream. The air was still and all I could hear was the water bubbling past and the birds that were gliding by overhead – music to my ears.

I held the box with Billy's remains and gave thanks for my loyal, unconditional friend and companion that he was to me. I sprinkled his ashes into Mother Ganga with gratitude and love and just watched them return to source as they dissolved into the flowing river. Tears of sadness and joy rolled down my cheeks. In spite of the mixed emotions, it was a special day as it was a profound experience of release and healing.

I then had a strong sense that I had to enter the river physically to cleanse myself of the pain and let go all that no longer served me. I immediately removed my kurti and stepped into the holy river as I was, in purple tank top and black leggings, and immersed myself in the crystal-clear, cool running waters, letting everything go ... the hurts I had experienced, the anger at myself for what I allowed, the love losses I mourned and, most of all, the old Jo, who for so long, was consumed with a Disease to Please. That girl was no more.

As I stood waist-deep in the river I absorbed the enormity of actually being at one with this Mother River and all she represented. I cupped water in my hands and drank it. It was like nectar – soft, sweet, fresh and gentle. I had never tasted water like this. It felt so soothing and energising. I looked around in awe of where I was. With the backdrop of the Himalayas, I closed my eyes and listened to the sound of the river and felt the sun soaking into my skin. It felt so cleansing, nourishing and invigorating. What a gift! As I stepped out of the water and sat in the sun to dry I felt a deep gratitude and joy for being here and for all I was experiencing.

I wrapped my shawl around my waist and started to explore the village towards the confluence of Mother Ganga and the Yamuna River. As I ambled through the tiny cobbled streets with crooked hand-built walls embedded with ancient traditions, I could feel the sacredness of my experience. The sense of peace and calm that came over me was immeasurable.

I was quite hungry by now and decided to pause at a corner food stall where a warm and welcoming mama was cooking one of my favourite simple meals, dahl dosa (Indian pancake with curried lentils). As I stood savouring the symphony of flavours and my surrounds, I saw an old man across the cobbled lane, sitting in the doorway to what I later discovered was his "healing home". I was intrigued and was drawn to him somehow. It was just one of those feelings that I instinctively needed to follow.

After my delicious dahl, I crossed over to explore more.

When I approached him, I noticed on the door behind him, in scraggly writing clinging to worn paint, a sign that said: Ayurvedic astrologer. My curiosity drew me closer and I asked him, with accompanying hand gestures, if he would do a reading for me. He stood up, bowed his head with his gnarled hands in prayer position and gestured me through the buckled wooden door into the tiny, dark room. He lit incense and a solitary candle, which he placed on a wobbly wooden table between us and motioned me to sit on the chair opposite him. He placed a pencil and paper in front of me so I could make notes, and finally settled down.

He looked intently into my eyes as if he could see into my soul. I felt a little awkward because I didn't know what he was looking for or seeing. All he asked me was my place and date of birth and time I was born. In just a few moments he was unpacking my life in detail, as if he had been intimately part of it. He shared his insights into what lay on my horizon. I watched him with fascination – his small droopy eyes and wizened face were somehow comforting. I knew there was no agenda other than the truth of what he was sharing with me. His reading was nothing short of eye-opening.

What this old man told me was beyond believable. He was halfway round the world from where I lived, and culturally completely different. His English was limited, yet he was accurately telling me things and referencing people that only people close to me would know about. He went as far as telling me I would marry again. As much as I baulked at the idea, he was adamant it was someone I already knew who travelled over many lands. I would meet him again in the next month. There was no room for doubt or scepticism, just my fear to believe it could be true. I knew who a groom could be but didn't want to acknowledge it to him, let alone myself. He was unshakable in his forecast. I was flabbergasted, excited, nervous and scared. I couldn't believe what my ears were hearing. I left there with a lot of other incredible insights that were relevant and my heart was aflutter. I couldn't wait to tell Tracey and Antonella. I knew they would be overjoyed.

I left the Vedic astrologer with a lightness in me and meandered down the hill into the main village in almost a dream state. I crossed the bridge over Mother Ganga deep in thought, appreciating the sun on my face and the river beneath me, feeling joy and peace in my heart. I heard a familiar voice, "Hello Sista." I turned to see it was Pavan, with his warm, welcoming smile beckoning me to come over to his store.

Pavan owned a little spiritual shop I visited a number of times while I was in Rishikesh. I liked him and had bought some significant pieces for myself and gifts for my girls, Tracey and Antonella. I passed by almost every day and I would stop by to say hello, so I felt like a regular.

On this day he took me by surprise. He wasn't just wanting to say hello or see if there would be something else I might be interested in buying (now that he knew my shopping style). Hand gestures and his broken English suggested he was asking me to come home to eat with his family. He pointed to a photo of his wife and son on a shelf behind him to help me understand. I was both taken aback and honoured that he would invite me to a meal with his family. I graciously accepted.

Before I could even ask him where I needed to go and when he would be expecting me, he stepped out from behind the counter and rolled down the shutters behind me. Suddenly I was closed inside the shop with him. I was a little confused and felt awkward until a moment later he was back behind the counter and pulled open a curtain behind him.

A whole world opened – his world. In a small open courtyard, his wife and son sat around a fire. A stainless steel pot rested on a stand above the flames. I ascertained that this was their midday meal, as the fragrance of spices from the steaming pot permeated the air. Pavan introduced me to his wife and son. They bowed their heads in reverence and I did the same. Without speaking, we looked each other in the eyes with an unspoken warmth. I then took both their hands in mine as a gesture of thanks for their hospitality. This heartfelt connection was mutual, confirmed by the look in their eyes and the lingering firmness of our holding hands. It reminded me of the quotes by Piglet and Pooh:

Piglet: "How do you spell Love?"

Pooh: "You don't spell it you feel it."

I sat on the floor on a cushion offered to me, between him and his son. His wife, Shanita, handed me a plate with a generous helping of ice and vegetable dahl. It was a delicious meal, shared with love and acceptance, that I savoured in silence. Eye contact was the language of communication.

The emotion that arose inside me each time I looked into their eyes moved me deeply. The special connection around this intimate circle was a heartfelt gift and left me in awe of the Universe's magic. Nothing was said but so much was spoken by our eyes. It was true connection without question or hesitation, through a feeling of acceptance and appreciation of each other. I was humbled that people with so little could give so generously – their heart, their time, their food and a share of their home space without expectation other than to just be together. This was a lesson that "little things are the big things". The value of this experience was beyond measure and one of many highlights on my journey. The memory is indelibly imprinted on my heart.

My personal pilgrimage to India was unlike any of my other overseas travels. They were filled with adventures, explorative experiences, and enjoying time with friends. This was more of an inner journey that left me with clarity in my thoughts; fullness and love in my heart; lightness in my spirit; and renewed energy in my body. It was the first big thing I had done for me – a truly meaningful gift to give to myself. I felt enriched and empowered to move forward in my life with more consciousness and confidence. I was aware of the choices and actions I needed to take in all areas of my life and I was vehement about being true to me, no matter what.

MEETING MY MATCH – CAMEL MAN

I returned home to South Africa with a bounce in my step as though I was unstoppable. Even a colleague who knew some of my story said, "Wow, you look effervescent. I have never seen you shine so brightly, Jo. It's as though you have done some sort of emotional shedding; spring cleaning and cleansing ..."

Hearing that from someone who didn't know me as intimately as my friends who have known me through all my life experiences, was revealing. I looked so different from the way I did before I left for India. I felt light, free and inspired.

I found a new rhythm to my life at home, seeing it through new eyes, and my soul was wide awake. Even when I returned to work my energy was more buoyant.

It was November 2016, a significant time in history. Donald Trump became the US president-elect after defeating Hillary Clinton, and Fidel Castro died. I was in Nelspruit for the week, running a change management workshop for one of my corporate clients when I received a phone message from an old friend. I was surprised and delighted when I read he was coming to Jo'burg and wanted to visit me. It was an unusual long-distance friendship and we hadn't seen each other in years.

Paul and I met in the spring of 2008 when Hurricane Gustav lashed the US Gulf Coast (Caribbean Sea). It was the 50th birthday celebration of a mutual friend of his and my ex. The party was being hosted on a farm in a barn decorated in a Greco-Roman theme. We were all required to dress in togas. I was not looking forward to it at all. I knew it would be a drinking bender and braced myself for a long night.

On the night of the party, as I approached the buffet table to make my selection for dinner, a tall stranger with dark hair, a kind face and warm smile introduced himself to me. He reached out his hand to greet me, "Hi, my name is Paul."

He looked me directly in the eye.

We immediately got chatting while serving our meal and he asked if he might sit with me. My ex joined and said, "Hi Paul, how are you doing?" To my surprise the two men knew each other, but I hadn't heard about this man before.

During our conversation, I came to understand that Paul was living in the UK. His wife was a doctor and was unable to make the party and he was in SA for only a short while on a brief visit. We found ourselves in deep and meaningful conversations about life and what it teaches you, sharing experiences on things that were important. What I noticed was that Paul was an intent listener, which was unusual in my experience of men. Throughout the time we spoke, he seemed extremely interested in what I had to say and looked deeply into my eyes. This was unusual for me as I often felt invisible. It was also a little unsettling, to say the least.

Whilst the rest of the guests were drinking, dancing and enjoying the celebration, we continued our exchange of thoughts and philosophies. Before we knew it, we heard someone say it was 2 a.m. Wow! The evening flew by and the remaining party players were starting to wind down and drift off to their various cottages for the night. It was certainly way past my bed time so Paul and I said goodnight. It felt like I had been talking to an old friend for hours. From a party I was dreading going to, it turned into a wonderful evening of substance and connection.

The next morning I was packing up to go home while my ex went down to the farm dam to store our boat. Suddenly I heard voices calling with a sense of urgency. I went outside to see what the commotion was about and I saw my ex's Land Rover had come to a halt en route back up from the dam. It looked as if something had gone badly wrong with it. I then heard voices shouting: "Call Paul, call Paul!"

I had no idea of any relevance or connection between Paul and a broken down Land Rover. I saw Paul emerge from the main house, striding purposefully towards the vehicle with a bag in his hand. I realised he was being called to rescue the situation. I had no idea, from the myriad of conversations we had explored the evening before, that he was in any way handy at vehicle breakdowns. More than an hour later Paul surfaced from under the vehicle covered with grease and dirt with a reassuring smile that all was well.

I was flabbergasted when I heard him turn to my partner and say, "You can count yourself lucky this happened here on the farm, because if this had happened when you were on the road back to Jo'burg, you and Jo would have been killed. My ex was visibly shocked at Paul's comment and thanked him profusely. I took Paul's hand and shook it with both my hands and said, "Thank you so much, I am so grateful you could help us. I had no idea that there was this dimension to you as well".

Paul responded with his big warm smile and said with care and his comforting warmth, "I'm glad I was here to help. Travel home safely."

We left feeling relieved that we were safe to go home but my soul felt restless. I knew why. I had the gift of meeting the kind of person I didn't think existed. It had been for such a brief time. I would have loved to know this kind of soul more. I was lost in my thoughts most of the way home, wondering if I would ever get to see this truly amazing human being again.

Then a thought crossed my mind which I shared with my ex, "You know, I think it would be a nice gesture to have our friends over for dinner, before they all fly out together, to say 'thank you' for the party at the farm, and perhaps have Paul over at the same time to thank him for fixing our vehicle."

He responded positively with, "Yes, good idea, set it up."

So it was agreed that two days later, on the Tuesday, our friends would come around for dinner with Paul. I was so looking forward to seeing him and having more time to connect with this uniquely kind and caring soul who was seemingly oceans deep.

It was a refreshing summer's evening in November and

I had prepared a lovely meal to be enjoyed in our garden. Our friends arrived with Paul and it was as though no time had passed. Paul and I picked up on the conversation threads we had begun a few evenings earlier, while the others continued having different conversations. Towards the end of the evening, while the others were immersed in their banter and chatter, Paul helped me clear the dinner table. He followed me into the kitchen, and as we put the dishes down, he turned to me, looked me directly in the eyes and said, "You are a very special lady and we have a very special connection."

I was at a loss for words. I could feel tears in my eyes that a stranger could see so deeply into my heart and soul and recognise my essence in such a short time. Being truly seen was rare for me. I felt a sadness that I would probably never see him again.

He continued, "If you are ever in the UK, let's have lunch."

As he said that, we both looked at each other and knew this would not be a good idea and could not happen, as we were both in relationships. It was a principle above all else, no matter what kind of relationships we were in. The ramifications were unthinkable, so we said goodbye and my heart was heavy.

I shared my plight with Antonella and Tracey and Antonella immediately said, "Trust the Universe, it works in mysterious ways, you don't just meet someone like that randomly. There is a bigger picture that we cannot yet see and this is not your last stop."

I remained distracted for weeks after the encounter. One afternoon I was on Facebook checking in to see what was happening in the worlds of my friends and bingo! A friend request was waiting for me in Messenger. It was from Paul.

This boosted my spirits dramatically. I was reassured that I was not out of sight, out of mind.

Even if this was the only form of connection we had, I was content. I updated my girls on this exciting occurrence and how delighted I was that Paul had reached out. As life went on and Antonella witnessed the ups and downs of my relationship with my ex, she would say, "My dear Jo, this is not your last stop, there is another future for you that is not yet apparent."

Paul and I remained Facebook friends for a number of years. He would always wish me happy birthday and merry Christmas. It was a year later, when some of the friends from the farm were at our home watching the 2010 FIFA World Cup. I overheard them from the kitchen saying that Paul was going through a rough time on every conceivable level. Of course, my ears pricked up and I was saddened when I heard the extent of what he was experiencing and the pain he was enduring. He was immigrating to Australia and selling his home and his business in the UK. His father had passed away from cancer and his cat had also passed on. All of this unfolded within the space of a year and culminated in him facing a devastating divorce.

As I listened to the conversation, all I could think of was how alone he must be feeling. I felt compelled to contact him via email. I extended my hand in friendship, as a support and safe place where he could share without feeling any judgement, and receive comfort and compassion. He so appreciated the care and I was glad I could be there for him as a trusted friend. We continued our email connection while he was navigating through his pain and making sense of the life changes that had been imposed on him in all directions.

Eight months later I received news from Paul that he was coming to SA for a school reunion and he was passing through Jo'burg. He would like to meet up for a cup of coffee. Guess what? I was on the blower to my girls to share my excitement. My frustration was Paul was now single and I was still in my ever-deteriorating relationship with my ex. In spite of it unravelling, I would not cross that line. Karma is something I take very seriously and I don't want to do to someone what I don't want done to me.

I was meeting him after one of my workshops in a quiet coffee shop. I made sure I was dressed to be remembered, in a three-quarter length, narrow-fitting black skirt with a flare at the bottom and a white sleeveless top with a crossover neckline – elegant and feminine – with reasonably high heels that were befitting. I even sprayed on my special Chanel perfume that was my signature. I felt good and knew he would approve. My stomach was like a kaleidoscope of butterflies. When we saw each other it was a magical feeling, although we both remained contained. We hugged tightly and with caution, the warmth of his hug was like a strong, comforting blanket that enveloped me and the smell of his skin seeped deep into my soul.

We settled down to catch up on his world and mine for the short time allowed. Paul was in SA for only a brief while. He was then going back to Australia to finalise his divorce and then to take a year to ride his bike through Africa before deciding what to do with his life. So we said goodbye again with the inevitable bear hug that I savoured, a kiss on the cheek and a heavy heart once more, never to know when we would see each other again. He needed to find answers to his life and my relationship was rapidly disintegrating. Neither of us needed further complications.

Once again, Antonella and I had our team talk about Paul, whom she had now nicknamed "Camel Man" (as Paul went on countless overland expeditions around the world and participated in the Camel Trophy, an off-road challenge, like the Olympics of 4x4). I shared in micro-detail how the coffee meeting went and I remember asking her, "Why is he now single and available and I am still stuck?" To which she wisely answered, "Because you both have inner work to do to clear yourselves and now is not the time. Patience ..."

This didn't console me even though I knew in my heart of hearts that where we both were would be a recipe for disaster. We would both be dragging the debris of our broken relationships into a new relationship that would be contaminated by our pasts.

Paul and I remained in contact and continued wishing each other happy birthday and merry Christmas over the next couple of years. Paul did not end up travelling through Africa on his bike. He met up with someone at his school reunion and fell into a relationship, which turned out to be a gift. It brought him back home to South Africa, back to his roots, and helped him decide to settle in Cape Town.

It was the beginning of 2016, a few months after I had left my ex. It was the start of a new life for me and a time that marked the end of a musical era. Musical icons, David Bowie, Prince and George Michael transitioned from this life. I went to Cape Town to a retreat with my mentor, Jevon, with whom I had studied HNLP in 2008. It was the best place for me to start piecing my life back together, clearing my mind clutter and reconnecting with myself in the safe cocoon of Hout Bay. The sea has always been a happy, healing place where I could breathe in life, restore my energy and feel the freedom of being me.

I knew Paul was in Cape Town and it was an opportunity to catch up on our lives. I messaged him that I would be there and he eagerly responded with some suggestions. We set up a time to meet for breakfast before the workshop started, on the first day of my retreat.

This time the tables were reversed and I was sharing my torrid tale of woes. Paul was visibly horrified by what I told him. As I almost expected, he jumped into the role the trusted friend, offering support, kindness and help from his own experience, and from a genuine place of care. It was a brief hour that we had and, as was customary in our rendezvous, we said goodbye with the hug and kiss on the cheek. This time I was just grateful to have him as my friend and a man who genuinely cared about me and wanted to help me, without any agenda. I was too raw to be thinking of possibilities with anyone, let alone Paul, and he was now in a relationship, which put him out of bounds.

You guessed it … I was on the phone to Antonella with the current updates and once again her comforting wisdom followed with, "Jo let him do this relationship thing, while you first find your way back to yourself and re-establish who you are and what you want. You need to be clear of everything. Take this time to focus on your healing. The timing is not now. Just trust ..."

I immersed myself in my retreat, remembering why I was there – to declutter me, recalibrate, reset and heal me. By the end of that long weekend, I was feeling lighter within myself. I left with a renewed vision, a clear path was set and I was focusing on being with me first, before entertaining joining paths with another. I was not recycling my past by escaping to distractions. No more!

The next phase of my "Journey to Me" was my personal pilgrimage to India – my gift to myself. This long-awaited experience was on the horizon and I now had a clear road ahead to make it happen, without encumbrances or responsibilities to hold me back or complicate my life. This gave me a bounce in my step, a sense of freedom in my soul. Nothing and no one was holding me back – not even a relationship.

Six months after my breakfast with Paul, the day before my birthday in August, I received my happy birthday message from Paul. This time it came a bit earlier than the actual date, as he was off on an expedition to the US. I excitedly responded that I was also going on my own expedition to India. He was both intrigued and happy for me. He wished me a wonderful trip and said he would love to hear all about it when I returned.

Just a few months later in November, on a hot Mpumalanga day I was in Nelspruit running a workshop again, still on a high from my travels through India. I was feeling as though heavy boulders had been lifted from my shoulders. I was crystal clear in my thoughts and laser focused on the life I wanted for myself. I was in an empowered place within me; I had taken charge of my life. I made my dreams a reality. I had taken "the road less travelled" and was happy with me and being with me. I didn't need distractions or a relationship to keep me occupied or validated. I loved being in my home with my fur companion, Winston, after Billy's passing in May. My life was simple and peaceful and that was enough for me.

Work was going well, my treasured tribe, my girls, were my family and I was content.

When I noticed a message from Paul on my phone my stomach was aflutter and my mind began to race. So much for being calm and centred.

"I am in Jo'burg. Can we get together on Friday night for dinner?"

"I am so sorry. I am out of town for a few days and will be driving back on Friday afternoon and will only be home around six," I responded.

He immediately answered, "No problem at all. I will wait for you and bring dinner. Just think about what you would like to eat and I will pick up some wine. Let me know your preference."

I was taken aback and at a loss for words, excited and nervous. Those butterflies were partying in my belly. I needed to refocus on the rest of the week's workshop. I didn't know what this would mean but I wasn't going to stop it either. These sporadic meetings over the years were not just coincidence, surely?

I knew he was still in a relationship and I had no intention of adding any complexities to his or my life – nothing was worth that. But the Curious Cat in me couldn't let this opportunity go.

My tribe, Antonella and Tracey, were the first to hear the news. Of course, they were in suspense and on standby for the next episode in the tale of Camel Man. They were cheering me on to follow my heart with caution.

On a balmy Friday evening I set the table on the veranda and Paul arrived at seven as arranged, with dinner in hand and a bottle of wine. It was an easy-flowing evening as it always had been when we connected over the years – as if no time had passed. He was eager to hear all about India. He listened attentively and I was bubbling to share it all. We had a wonderful time exchanging travel stories and experiences. It was great to share a comfortable exchange with this kind, caring soul who was truly interested in what I had to say. We spoke about the things that mattered most in life and where I was since I had last seen him eight months prior, when I was in tatters after I exited my marriage. I mattered to him. This was also a first for me.

As the evening drew to a close, I had to ask Paul a question that had been gnawing at me since he arrived for dinner. Although he had his usual warm, welcoming smile, there appeared to be a heavy cloud over his head. His eyes seemed dimmer than I had seen before, his eyelids were heavy, as though his light was being snuffed out. So I jumped in, "Okay, so we have spoken at length about all the fun travels and experiences we have both had but I need to know, how are you really? How is your life in Cape Town? You seem flat in your energy. Something is missing ..."

He was seemingly taken aback by my observation but slowly told of the struggles and pain he had been enduring in the relationship. We spoke a long while as we unpacked his life and circumstances. It broke my heart to see the deep sadness in this beautiful soul who always showed up to help everyone with kindness and warmth.

Through the lengthy conversation we had, he arrived at some harsh realisations. They were not easy to face and had been nudging him quietly inside. They were difficult to digest but would ultimately lead to a decision he would need to make about his future. I felt sad that he had to navigate more pain again. Before he left, I reassured him I would walk alongside him as his friend and I gave him a book by a Buddhist monk, Thich Nhat Han called True Love, to help him through his turmoil. I felt intuitively that it would bring some insights into his life and give him confidence to take the decisions that would best serve him.

As he walked out the door, he turned to me with his sad yet twinkling eyes and said, "I have food for thought, a book to read and a decision to make. I will see you in January."

I messaged my girls the updates soon after he left. Although I had an inkling as to what he meant, I was not going to make any assumptions that it included me. I was not going to set myself up for any disappointment and let my mind run away with me. I needed to leave him to his path and not be derailed from mine. I did admit to the girls that there was bubbling hope in my heart even though my head was saying, "Get on with your life and stay on your track. What will be will be – let it be." They both responded with the same words: "Patience. It is all unfolding. Just trust."

I was determined to remain true to me and avoid old traps that had derailed me. I was not steering the river in my need for love again and I was not adding to my karma that I was working off. I was still working on my inside-out job and rewiring my mind to form new habits of behaviour for a better, stronger, and congruent me.

Although Paul had said he would see me in January, two months later, I didn't know when and where either of us would be on our paths. My focus right then was on the next phase of my Journey to Me and I felt proud of my commitment to myself. This was new for me. I had signed up with Davidji and was about to start my mindfulness and meditation teacher training. It was a six-month learning journey that required deep inner work and intense focus, before I headed off to do my final week in residence in Carlsbad, San Diego. The programme was my priority and the perfect way to reinforce my commitments to me and the life I was choosing. So I immersed myself in my lessons. Recycling my past was not an option.

True to his word, Paul called me in mid-January when I least expected it. He was coming up to Jo'burg again and asked if we could meet at the end of the month. I had now been out of my marriage for a year and was in a completely different space within myself. My life had truly changed for the better and I was more ME. I gladly accepted as I was curious to find out what had transpired in his life since our time together in November. I was preparing to go to the US to have time with my dear friend Michele in California, before my week with Davidji, and I was excited to share my plans with Paul.

I cooked dinner for us at home so we could chat freely and as long as we liked, without interruptions. Paul wasted no time as we sat down with a glass of wine before dinner and gave me the news that he had reached the end of his relationship and could no longer continue in something that ceaselessly eroded who he was. He was moving out.

I was quietly excited but with caution, as this did not necessarily mean his next step was with me. I reined my racehorse back into her stable and maintained focus on my immediate next steps. Part of my learning was to trust in Divine order and Divine time preordained by the Universe. As Dr Wayne Dyer always said, "Let Go and Let God".

The timing of my trip was perfect to give him the space and time he needed to clear his path. With that, we concluded our evening. Paul wished me well on my journey to the US. He would see me in March on my return. Until then, he was going on an expedition and then moving to his own place. We would connect then.

My lessons continued in patience. I listened to my gut and trusted the Universe that all is in Divine order, remaining true to me and my values. I focused on what was important to me: being able to live with my choices with comfort and confidence, and accepting that everything was as it should be and everything always works out for the best in the end.

I truly believe that when you do the right things, the right things happen.

My granny always said, "Joey, you teach people how to treat you, so start the way you intend to carry on. Things don't go wrong, they start wrong."

So this time, somehow, goodbye to Paul felt different from the way it had ever been before. It felt open-ended, not final. That in itself had to produce a different result, didn't it?

ADVENTURE LIFE WITH CAMEL MAN

It was two years on since I exited my marriage I was now 54, I had lost my cortisol belly and bum and was the slimmest I had been in 10 years. My hair was growing thicker again. My blonde mane was back. I felt light in my being – mentally, emotionally and, of course, physically. My spiritual life was restored and strong, which made me so happy. My mind was clear, my emotions were balanced and my gut was quiet. I was feeling great when I woke up every day and I liked me again. I was back to my consistent commitment to my daily rituals. Meditation and yoga were daily practices that kick-started my day. Journaling my gratitude before bed was how I sealed the day before sleep.

For the first time in my life I felt I was living my life my way – in my truth. I had inner peace that I had not known for most of my life. I had sample tastes of it over the years but with no consistency or longevity. Now it was something I was waking up to and going to bed with every day. I was no longer squeezing in or secretly finding time for me. It was now a way of life for me. I was having fun. I was laughing again. I finally felt fearlessly free to be me.

I had moved my life to Cape Town to settle down with my Camel Man and it truly was a dream come true. I finally found the deepest and truest love I had ever known and long wished for all my life. I was living at the beach in my soul's ultimate happy place, with my beloved furkid, Winston.

Life was about to become an adventure because part of making a life with Camel Man was wanting to understand the elements that made up his life – his overland expeditions and the classic car rallies to which he gave technical support. This was the year to dive into both, to experience his world and understand what made up this wonderful human being.

What a ride it was! It was a steep learning curve when the unimaginable happened in both.

I began my year by participating in a classic car rally around South East Asia, an event for which wealthy car lovers ship their classic cars to exotic destinations to drive them along scenic routes through remote areas past the most spectacular views, staying in the most luxurious places. I was excited and delighted at the prospect of another adventure into the unknown. I knew it would be a growing and expansive experience and one that Camel Man always said "was fun". How that would look was what I didn't know and could not have anticipated. As is true to my nature, I jumped into the deep end and had to figure things out as I went along. I guess that was part of the adventure for me.

It was a gruelling but mind-boggling experience. The 40 participants plus crew mostly knew each other and were part of a friendship group of ralliers in their 60s and 70s. Camel Man had rallied with them all over the world for more than 16 years. I was the new kid on the block as Camel Man's partner (previously they had rallied with his ex-wife, who was the rally doctor). What caught us both off guard was how unwelcome I was made to feel by many of the participants, even though it was agreed that I would join as part of the support team, with a defined role. My welcome at the briefing dinner was from one of the wives, who had known Camel Man for all these years of rallying. She called me aside with a cautionary tone and said, "I hope you know how lucky you are to have this man in your life. I just want to make sure you understand that you need to take very good care of him, especially after all he went through with his ex-wife. Just make sure you appreciate what you have and look after him, otherwise you will have me to reckon with." She offered a wry smile and then swanned off.

What just happened? I thought. And who is this witch judging me without knowing me and thinking she is Camel Man's fairy godmother and saviour? Who on earth does she think she is and what right has she to even think she has an opinion that matters in my life? Another condescending individual who thinks she can lord it over me, as some insignificant waif. She doesn't know a thing about me – nor did she even ask – she has just assumed the role of Camel Man's protector.

The shock of this unwarranted lecture rendered me speechless. I gave her a tentative, uneasy smile and could feel my eyes almost coming out on stalks.

I ruminated over this inappropriate instruction and thought, if this is how it's going to be, this is going to be an extremely long and hard six weeks. In addition, her husband, who was one of the rally organisers, was also quite dismissive of me. What a way to start, I thought.

I chose to put it to the back of my mind and focus on the bigger picture of why I was on the trip. I really wanted to enjoy the experience. The build-up was exciting and I was not going to allow six weeks to be wrecked because of one person's ego. This was a long-awaited trip to places I had never seen and I was not giving power to someone else to ruin this for me.

We started in Hoi An in Vietnam, then moved onto Cambodia, Thailand, Myanmar (Burma), Laos and back into Vietnam, to Hanoi. The rallies really are about adventure travel, not races. The route was pre-set (after being recce'd) and we were on the road every day, moving to a new town. We made a couple of two-night stops but the days began at sunrise and finished before dusk in each new town or country.

For the crew, the rally day starts before the participants leave and ends after dinner. It is not a paid holiday by any means. You are showing up all day, every day, with little or no down time to rest or shed your mask.

Camel Man's focus was to attend to the cars' mechanical issues either along the way or at the next stop. He was constantly making a plan, finding solutions or improvising, as workshops equipped for classic cars were limited in this part of the world. He loved the challenge. The locals were always willing and helpful and welcomed this the experience as a highlight in their lives and villages. Many of them had never seen classic cars.

I thoroughly enjoyed connecting with the local people in each country, the beautiful scenery, and the sensational local food. I loved the markets when we had a chance to explore them and, of course, supported them by buying memories to take home.

The journey was tough – not only because of the rough roads and the mountainous terrain but I had to dig deep within myself to face the resistance and disdain daily from a number of the participants. I always had to remind myself why I was on the trip – that it was a learning experience and to support Camel Man. Most of all I was working on avoiding the pattern of people-pleasing for approval. This was a slippery slope.

Camel Man could see my struggle and felt compassion for me. I was not only far from home but totally out of my comfort zone in an unfamiliar environment with total strangers, doing something I had never done before. My heart was heavy. He was caught between a rock and a hard place and hugely annoyed at how I was being treated. He had not experienced this before with these travellers.

The days were long. Ill-prepared vehicles often required his time on the road and, though we arrived at hotels late at night, he sometimes still had to work on other cars that needed attention before they could proceed the next day. The work was relentless and exhausting. He also had to navigate human dynamics when drivers were stressed and frazzled about their wonky vehicles. So he had his hands full and not a lot of time for us.

This is what adventure rallying was all about – the challenge, endurance and resilience. The fun was exploring new places and cultures with these old classics and testing their durability. But for the crew it was 24/7 work.

We were halfway through the rally in Thailand, about to cross into Myanmar when Camel Man developed a hacking cough and tight chest. Being who he is, he forged on regardless.

He had to deal with a participant who had erroneously put petrol into a diesel tank. Fortunately, he resolved it before any damage was done and we entered Myanmar that afternoon.

By the time we arrived at the first hotel in Myanmar, Camel Man was sweating and not feeling great.

I said, "Love, you need to go to bed and the other cars can wait ..."

He was insistent and, out of character, he snapped, "No, I have to see to the other cars. I can't just leave them."

I felt helpless and alone. I just watched in despair as he walked away. I knew he was on a slippery slope with his health. Then suddenly he stopped and turned around slowly. He was shivering and I went over to him and he succumbed.

"Let's put you to bed – a warm shower, hot soup, Med-Lemon and some good rest."

I put my arm around his shaky body and led him to our room. I warded off participants who intercepted us with their car troubles and told them he would not be available till the morning. Quite shocking was the entitled attitude of some who expected to have their cars seen to without any consideration for the obvious situation with Camel Man.

He woke in the morning feeling no better and I became more and more concerned. He had sweated in the night. He still had a temperature, his chest was burning and his cough was not improving. There was no way it would be possible for him to drive and we would need to make a plan with our truck. I was not comfortable driving on these difficult roads and the challenging terrain of vertical mountain climbs, steep drops, and rough, raw and remote winding roads, some of which had been freshly cut ahead of us.

We decided that the logistics director would drive our truck with me and the rally doctor would drive the logistics truck. Paul would then be moved to the next stop, Naypyidaw, in an ambulance (which is mandatory as part of the logistical support on these events). Access to hospitals is not freely available in these remote areas.

Seeing Paul being strapped to the stretcher under a warm blanket was terrifying, especially being so far from home and anything familiar. I was drawing on all my resources and knowledge to figure out ways to help him get relief and feel better. His breathing was laboured because of the congestion and I was boiling water and adding eucalyptus oil so he could nebulise and open his airways. I was doing reflexology on his feet with Tiger Balm to clear his body of toxins and to help unblock his Eustachian tube and sinuses. I rubbed Vicks on his back to give his lungs relief. I was bathing his forehead and behind his neck with cold hand-towels to reduce the fever. To get him to eat was difficult, as he was nauseous from the mucous running down his throat. He had no appetite, but we couldn't afford for him to get any weaker. I was pouring Rehydrate into him twice a day to keep him hydrated and giving him Panado to alleviate the pain.

I was desperate. We were in a foreign country and none of my go-to resources were accessible to me, like our homeopath, doctor, acupuncturist or pharmacy, let alone family and friends. With the exception of the crew, I was surrounded by uninterested and disdainful participants. I was frightened and alone as he was just getting worse, drifting in and out of hallucinations from the fever and then going into wracking shivers. Then he would break into a hacking cough that was soon followed by a coughing fit, to the point of vomiting. This was beyond an adventure now. It was fast becoming a nightmare.

When I asked the doctor for some medical relief for Paul he said, "Just keep doing what you are doing – it's a virus, like any flu. Keep him hydrated and comfortable and it will pass."

By the time we got to the hotel in Naypyidaw, the capital of Myanmar, I saw the writing on the wall. I implored the doctor for antibiotics as I was watching Paul slip away fast and with all the other intermediary over-the-counter meds and alternative potions we carry on our travels, he was not getting any better. So he examined Paul, did all the necessary checks to ensure he was administering the medication appropriately and quietly uttered to me, "He has a temperature of 43 degrees and he is showing signs of bronchial pneumonia."

It took every fibre of my being to remain calm. The thought of Paul potentially going to hospital in a foreign country was horrific. Although our logistics director knew the ropes and was well connected in Myanmar, I was scared out of my wits at any prospect of Paul being hospitalised. So I was on a mission to get him better whatever it took and nothing or no one would stand in my way.

I managed to stabilise Paul after two doses of medication and a better night's sleep, and the next day we could move him to the next stop, Bagan, a city with the largest concentration of Buddhist Temples, pagodas and stupas in the world. It was beautiful, like a sea of temples, and we were thankfully based there for two days. After rest for two full days in one place, Paul turned the corner.

The medication had kicked in, he was sleeping better and starting to eat again. There was light at the end of this dark tunnel. By the time we were ready to move on to Inle Lake, Paul was better though not yet fully recovered. He was out of bed, walking around and taking it slowly. So we moved him from Bagan to Inle Lake by ambulance again, so he didn't need the pressure of driving. We were due to stay another two days, thankfully, so Paul could stabilise with some more rest. I was relieved.

The next day was a rest day and for the first time since we had arrived in Myanmar, I saw the light in Paul's eyes as he began returning to his old self. He was able to get up and join the experience on the lake, going through the raised flower gardens and enjoy watching the leg-rowing fisherman working their craft. I felt some relief, although I still watched him like a hawk.

The group of travellers were all absorbed in their adventures. I was shocked how totally removed they were and unaware of the severity of Paul's illness. Some would cordially check in, out of respect, but not with much real interest or care. However, there was a particular man, Neil, who did sensitise to our plight and was genuinely concerned about me and Paul. In his way he took me under his wing as he would a daughter, and was incredibly supportive and kind. He always ensured I had a place to sit with him and his co-driver at meals and would check in with me regularly to see if there was anything we needed.

It was comforting and reassuring to know there was someone in our corner. He kept me focused and always added his dry sense of humour to the mix, especially when I thanked him for his care and kindness: "Well, I can't be Paul's nurse so I'll be your watch dog."

After our two-day respite at Inle, Paul was able to continue driving. He had not by any means gained full strength but he managed to keep a gentle pace.

Our first stop for the day was Mount Popa, a breakfast spot overlooking the majestic volcano. However, our arrival there had been delayed, as we had stopped to help a young man who had been knocked off his motorbike. Never a dull moment. By the time we got to the venue, most of the participants were already heading off, with the exception of one vehicle that had problems and needed Paul's help. Paul was doing okay and today was seemingly going to be a good day. So I thought.

While Paul was attending to the troubled car, one of the organisers came racing back to the breakfast spot in a rage. This, by the way, was the husband of the woman who had lectured me at the start of the rally. I had already heard mutterings on the two-way radios that the route book had an error and people were taking a wrong turn and becoming lost. He made a beeline for me and launched a barrage of accusations.

"Why did you not answer your phone?" he scolded me like a headmaster.

I politely answered, "I haven't had a minute to change

sim cards as we were dealing with an accident shortly after we left the hotel and then raced here to help the Rover."

He raised his voice in fierce reprimand, "I told you to put the sim card in immediately when I gave it to you at the car park and you disobeyed my instruction."

I was not going to tolerate being treated like a subordinate. "Who do you think you are speaking to? I am not your child and I don't work for you!"

He immediately flung back at me, "You will follow my orders on this rally or leave. Do you understand?"

I was so enraged that I was shaking. My blood was boiling. What I wanted to say to him was, "YOU messed up the route book and are so embarrassed in front of all your cronies that your fragile ego needs a punching bag, and bullying me is your outlet!"

That would have just made matters worse, so I chose the high ground.

I spun around and stormed off incensed as the tears just streamed down my cheeks in sheer exasperation. How the hell do I find these bully characters – do I have it written on my forehead, I cried inside.

I was exhausted and sleep-deprived from the nights of keeping vigil over Paul and the long driving days. I was worn out from worrying and fed up with walking on egg shells and dancing to the tune of these precious people. This was the final straw. All I wanted to do was get the hell out of this nightmare and go home. There was no fun in this trip at all. Frankly, this rallying business was, in my mind, for the birds. To be surrounded by self-serving people who didn't give a toss about Paul's well-being, and who felt a sense of entitlement from paying a lot of money, was too much. I couldn't be paid enough to put up with this kind of treatment. I was at my wits end.

When we were back on the road later I told Paul what had happened. He was furious. He had held back on reacting to earlier bad behaviour but this was the straw that broke the camel's back. He called for a meeting with the organisers and the logistics director, who had also had difficulties with the organisers. Paul demanded an apology from the organiser who barked at me. Paul gave him an ultimatum that if it ever happened again, we would both be leaving the rally. That stopped everyone in their tracks. They had never seen that side to Paul. With that, the organiser apologised reluctantly with a sheepish look and without making any eye contact.

The rally continued well. We saw some beautiful places and had some wonderful experiences. Paul was getting better day by day although he was still very tired and low in energy. I was completely drained and desperate to go home. To be so far away among indifferent strangers who showed no compassion was difficult and painful and something I was not able to digest. I had to continue reminding myself of the purpose of this trip. Paul was also caught off guard. Being so ill and witnessing my experiences had never happened to him before.

I made my contribution to the rally. It wasn't a free ride and I met myself in a very different environment. Yet another reminder to remain true to who I am and not regress into who I think I need to be to appease others. It was a tough test and clearly my learning was ongoing.

When the end of the rally came, there was much relief. Everyone was exhausted. There was much jubilation from an incredible adventure that was accomplished safely and it was celebration time. So I thought!

All the cars were being lined up in formation overlooking Halong Bay. The logistics director, from his position on the roof of a VW Combi bus, directed me where he wanted the cars so I could show the participants where to park. In the midst of this smooth-flowing operation, one of the other organisers came thundering towards me like a tornado and, without awareness of what was going on, said abruptly, "Why are you here? I have my plan and you don't know what you are doing!"

I was so gobsmacked that I could have slapped him. I pointed up to where the director was and snapped,

"I am following his instructions."

What I really wanted to say was, "Where the hell were you in the first place with your precious plan? Now you barge in with your position of self-importance and disrupt it all."

He further insulted me, in his bolshie way, "You need to mind your own business and stick to the things you are told to do."

Well, that was it. I walked away leaving them all to it. I walked over to Paul who watched this whole circus and said, "I cannot believe these are people you have rallied with for over 10 years and they behave like misogynists. Just because they have loads of money to travel exotically does not entitle them to treat people like the hired help or less. Money certainly doesn't buy class." I was livid but still had to find my smiley face somehow before the gala dinner that night in celebration of the completion of the rally. This was an adventure to hell and back.

At the end of it all, I learned that I needed to trust who I am more and care less whether they approved of me or not. None of them took the time and trouble to get to know me and they were not friends I needed to win over.

What was most comforting was the fact that although Neil had rallied with these people for more than a decade, he was equally appalled by their behaviour. Throughout the journey, particularly from the time of Paul's illness, he had my back and was incredibly supportive. He was my constant pillar of strength. We became firm friends from then on till he died in October 2022 – he was a true gift from the rally!

Paul was deeply disappointed by how the whole rally unfolded, because that was not how he had experienced them before. He was mortified that the people he had rallied with and thought he knew so well after all the years, could behave so disrespectfully. He had wanted me to have a positive experience and was sad that I had endured such a gruelling trip on so many levels. He drew a line in the sand, "When we travel together, people have to accept us as a team. If they don't value us, they don't deserve us. I will never tolerate this again – nothing is worth this. We are a team and they can take it or leave it!"

It was a first for me to be a united front with a partner, where I was valued and I mattered and, most of all, that our relationship was a priority. This was when I realised I had definitely shifted something in my life to have attracted someone who was aligned in values to who I am and what I stand for.

THE ADVENTURE CONTINUES ...

Four months later that year, we were set for another adventure. This one would be different and I was excited. It was an overland expedition around Southern Africa for a month in a 4X4 with a group of fellow travellers whom Paul had known for more than 10 years and had accompanied before. I was embarking on another element of Paul's life, meeting more of the people with whom he had journeyed through life, and I knew it would be an expansive experience. Little did I know that it, too, had a lesson in store for me.

It was mid-winter and Paul and I were meeting the posse in Botswana. As we drove, I sang along with Bradley Cooper and Lady Gaga to Shallow and we were in high spirits. Paul had travelled with the group leader extensively over a number of years on overland expeditions. I was looking forward to getting to know him as I had heard a lot about their overland adventures together.

It was a pleasant gathering for us to all to familiarise ourselves with one another. I felt a little apprehensive as you would when you have not done something before and were meeting people with whom you would travel for a month. I had not done this kind of travel before and found myself again being the new kid on the block among people who were old hands at this, and I didn't know anyone except Paul. Nonetheless I was eager for the learning experience, keen to participate and hopefully to be accepted by the group.

The next day we set off as the sun emerged over a cloudless horizon. There was a flurry of bird activity as we left the camp – chirping, twittering, tweeting and the ultimate birdsong, the glorious call of the African fish eagle. What a way to start the day ... welcome home we felt.

As we travelled Paul and I spoke about the different

personalities and how we expected the dynamics to unfold. I offered a suggestion based on the work that I do in team dynamics, "Love, how about we offer a campfire circle at sunset, while dinner is cooking, and chat about everyone's expectations and limitations? You know, like codes of conduct or group guidelines. It often gets more complicated when there are strangers in the mix. It can alleviate some uncomfortable situations and prevent any group dynamics that may arise unnecessarily."

"That's a great idea, let's try it and see what happens. It will be interesting to see how our leader takes it, as I am sure he has never done anything like this before. Neither have I …"

"Given how different we all are, emotionally, practically, intellectually, let alone culturally, it might iron out some creases early on. After all, this time there are five of us for one month not just you and him. Believe me, in close quarters it can get messy."

"Ok great – I like that idea. I'll set it up when we get to camp."

Paul did a great job of arranging it and gathering everyone around the fire, "Guys, we are all looking forward to this adventure and it would add value if we could all share our expectations and concerns so we can manage them constructively as a team."

That went down like a lead balloon. "We are all adults and know how to behave. If anyone has anything to say, we just say it and move on."

Paul and I looked at each other and dropped the idea like a hot cake. It was like immediately putting a lid on the pot. The conversation morphed into superficial banter. It left me with an uncomfortable niggle in my gut.

As the days followed, I was finding my rhythm with the logistics of this new way of travel. It was day and night from the lifestyle we enjoyed in many of the luxury hotels in South East Asia.

We would arrive at a camp site in the bush before dusk,

set up camp for the night and make a fire to cook our evening meal before the predators arrived on the hunt for burnt offerings. Our accommodation was a rooftop tent. We shared ablutions and lived out of a travel duffel bag on the back seat of the truck. I was getting the feel of living life on the road in a confined space with my partner and our truck was our home for the next month. Everything we needed, from clothes, water, ablutions and food, to bedding and furniture was in and around the truck for a month. Our overnight stops would be in different locations in the wild – no hotels, guesthouses or B&Bs or such comforts. This was real adventure stuff and I was ready for it.

At this early stage, I was just an observer, not volunteering much in the way of conversation, as it was very much about the group reconnecting, reminiscing and discussing the trip and plans for the month ahead. They were all old hands at overland travel in the wild and the trip was specifically intended as a filming project.

At sunset of the third day, with an amber sky reflecting the magical Savuti dusk, birds still chirping in a slight breeze, we had set up camp and the fire was crackling. The men were debating the technicalities of troublesome refrigeration in the leaders' vehicle. It was causing frustration. Was it the fridge, the electrics, operator error? I detected an underlying tension brewing.

The expedition leader has been known to be a controversial and volatile character at times. Paul, in his calm way, proposed that in the clearer light the next morning, they would investigate and take it from there. We enjoyed a delicious meal with some superficial chit chat underpinned by restraint.

Day Four was glorious. The air was crisp, the sky clear and the birds busy. There was a magical stillness. Dawn is my favourite time of day. Wherever I am in the world, I love to rise and make morning coffee for everyone and take mine to a spot where I can sit quietly to enjoy the peace and the promise of a new day.

I sat on a log, entertained by the hornbills picking up crumbs around the campsite and making friends with the local squirrels.

Paul and I enjoyed quiet time together before he joined the lads to continue the refrigeration debate and do the necessary investigation. I went back to the truck to do some housekeeping and heard the leader belt out, "I am telling you this is the manufacturer's fault and you don't know what the fek you are talking about."

I leapt to the doorway of the rooftop tent to see what was going on. The men were standing around the vehicle. Paul was trying to placate the situation and bring reason to the discussion. The leader vehemently denied any part he might have played and continued his tirade on the product. When Paul asked him another question to rule out all possibilities, he yelled, "Paul, I am not an idiot and you are talking bollocks."

Things were hotting up and squeezed my bully trigger. I couldn't listen to Paul being treated with disrespect and dodging profanities from someone behaving irrationally – it was abuse. Whichever way Paul tried to explain things to him from his expert experience, he would hear none of it and take no responsibility for any part he might have played in creating the situation.

I climbed down from the rooftop tent and high-tailed it over to the men without excusing my interruption. Wide-eyed with rage, I said slowly through gritted teeth, "What did I just hear you say?" The leader turned in shock to face me. I continued, "Who the heck do you think you are, talking to Paul in that way?"

My blood was boiling and I didn't care what the consequences would be. I would not allow this tirade to continue. We were at the beginning of the trip and if this kind of behaviour was allowed to continue, it would be a recipe for disaster. This time I was not keeping quiet the way I did in South East Asia.

"Paul is not your punching bag. If you can't speak with

respect then please don't speak at all."

The leader was stunned by my attack and, given how he glared at me, I imagined he would have loved to have hurled something back at me. Instead he spun on his heels and thundered off, leaving behind the sound of swishing grasses and crushing dry leaves.

I made Paul another cup of coffee and some breakfast so he could also catch his breath. He was shocked and angry at the injustice of it all. He had never been treated or spoken to like that, in all the years he and the leader had known each other. We spoke about it and I encouraged him to resolve it before it deteriorated any further. It required an apology – or the trip would be a disaster. Paul looked at me. "I see why it would have been important to set out some ground rules at the beginning and here we are, only four days in …"

Peace was made later that day. Yet I couldn't help feeling that there was a resounding resemblance to the South East Asia trip, where people with a certain sense of power (for whatever reason) deem it okay to treat people in a support role without respect and vent their frustrations while totally disregarding the impact of their actions.

Here we were again, the same situation in a different place. Therein lies the lesson once more. "Find your voice and speak your truth fearlessly."

A few days later when one member of the posse was flying out, the rest of the group went on to Lake Kariba for two days. When we arrived our rented boat was not available. Apparently nothing had been confirmed by the leader, so the boat company cancelled it. Again, tension arose. An alternative boat had to be arranged for us, which would take a few hours. This certainly added to my frustration, as I was having to find campsites on the fly most days, at the last minute in some remote parts of Botswana where vacant camping spots are not a dime a dozen.

In spite of some of the logistical bumps along the way, we were seemingly all coping well until we reached Mana Pools.

It was our last significant stop before the journey home. This is when it all finally blew up in biblical proportions.

We arrived at the campsite on the edge of the Zambezi River in all its glory. The sun was setting and we were reaching the golden hour, a film maker's power hour. The horizon was glowing amber, reflecting the ball of fire slowly setting. The majestic river was flowing steadily, and the birdsong was melodic and beautiful. Another solitary call of a fish eagle made Paul and me smile.

We set up camp and Paul and I went ahead, to light the fire and prepare the evening meal. None of our posse was in sight. The leader's friend was just ambling back from the ablutions, his head hanging in thought. We could feel something was off. Her said the leader had gone to bed. Now we definitely knew something was afoot.

Paul went to the leader's tent and asked him if he was okay. He grunted some inaudible response. Paul then more assertively said, "If you have something on your chest, let's have it out – this is not helpful to any of us. Let's hear what's on your mind, talk about it and resolve it. We are days away from the end and this is no way to wrap up the trip."

With that the leader burst out of his tent and marched to the fireside, with Paul following looking bewildered. He spun around in his bolshie way and yelled, "You want to know what's wrong, well I will tell you what's wrong!" And he proceeded to hurl the biggest load of hogwash imaginable and levelled unfounded accusations that sent us reeling.

"Yesterday you and Jo boarded the boat and took over without any consideration for the work I am here to do. You know the front of the boat is where the best footage is captured. You are both completely selfish and inconsiderate!"

We were stunned and I responded questioningly, "But I specifically asked you where you wanted to position yourself and you said it didn't matter. You said: 'It makes no difference'... and now you have turned this all back on us."

He immediately blurted back without taking any

responsibility (yet again) and continued distorting the incident, "Actually you have both just commandeered this whole trip as if it is yours."

This warped rampage was outrageous and deteriorating into a character assassination of Paul that left us shell-shocked. Paul was angry and shaking at the gall of it all. I was fizzing mad.

The more I listened, the more I became a raging lion inside, but I needed to maintain my dignity without sinking to his level of disrespect. I was done with these bullying tactics and abuse and was not going to hold back anymore. I had observed enough over three weeks and I had had a gut full. I was not going to endure another replay of our South East Asia scenarios. Anyone and everyone who knew Paul, including the leader, would know that the accusations levelled at him were far from the truth. There was clearly a thorn under his saddle. We just didn't know what it was.

The leader paced around the fire like a caged animal. I threw out a response, not giving a damn how he reacted. "How dare you speak to Paul in that way after all he has done for you to make this trip possible for your project? You wouldn't have had a vehicle to start with, if it weren't for him."

I could feel I was slipping into a tirade of destruction. I had had this man's egotistical, self- opinionated bullying bunk in chunks and I was going to cut him off at the knees. He just wasn't expecting it, because most people didn't stand up to him, let alone a female.

"Worst of all you have known Paul longer than most people, so you know damn well that what you are accusing him of is the furthest from the truth. You need a punching bag for all your frustration at the things that have gone sideways, including your incompetent planning, and you are abusing his good nature. You have an audience to play to. The difference is that he doesn't have an ego like you and has no need to fight back and try to win an argument. Don't mistake his silence for weakness. Whatever thorn is scratching you, deal with it. Don't use Paul and me as your convenient whipping boys because you can't be man enough to take responsibility for your actions. You have not planned this trip well, and responsibility for the things that have gone pear-shaped is pointing squarely at you. Paul keeps catching your dropped balls, with no appreciation, only blame. We keep covering your butt and you get to insult and humiliate him in front of an audience. What is wrong with you?"

Paul then jumped in and said with a shaky voice stifling his anger, "We would have had come unstuck with accommodation a number of times, had it not been for Jo's resourcefulness. She found places on the hoof because you had nothing organised, including the houseboat."

I took my final swing. "It has become very clear that you don't want me or us on this trip as you are stooping really low to find ways of discrediting us. So if this is how deep you have to dig that you are resorting to this level of behaviour, to get us to leave, we can help you out and move on in the morning."

He suddenly lowered his voice and with gritted teeth said, "That's entirely your decision – just remember if you leave, it's on your head and not on my hands – I never told you to leave."

I couldn't help myself and yelled back, "No, of course not. You are too much of a coward to own that, too, so you are using the pathetic art of provocation."

Paul interjected and in his usual calm and contained way said, "I think we need to leave this conversation, sleep on it and reconvene in the morning."

Without another word, everyone retired to their tents and Paul and I went to sit at the fire. We stared into the soothing flicker of the flames and listened to nature's evening orchestra as we let the evening wash away from us.

We sat under the sparkling Milky Way long into the night wrapped in blankets and drinking steaming coffee with Kahlua, while reflecting on what had happened. We couldn't believe how much from left field this avalanche had come, in the most twisted and disrespectful way. The shock of all shocks was that Paul and the leader had travelled many thousands of kilometres overland together and so knew each other well. For this to go so badly wrong was unfathomable.

By early hours of morning, we were truly deflated by the whole trip and I came to the conclusion, "My love, it doesn't matter if it is the King of England, the Dalai Lama or the Sultan of Brunei – no one gets away with treating us in that way, because we then have to accept what we allow. I am done with bullies and being fearful to speak up when something is glaringly unjust. Nobody died and made him God and everyone is scared to take him on. Well, we can't be paid enough to tolerate anyone's bullying tactics and be expected to stand by and allow it to happen. No more – not friends, family, colleagues, clients – no one. We teach people how to treat us."

When we rose the next morning we gathered round the fire for coffee and it was amicably decided we would all take time out for a couple of days. We would each travel on our own and meet up at Nata in Botswana, to then complete the trip.

When we finally met again three days later, it was an awkward reunion. It was superficial chatter about what we did on the days we spent apart. We clearly tolerated each other and were very eager to end the journey back in Windhoek. Till then, we all remained cordial.

Talk about an adventure. The physical and practical bits were the easy part even though at times there were challenges that needed navigation mentally and physically. What I soon realised was that the most complicated and unpredictable challenges were the humans, even more so with people you thought you knew.

This took adventure travel to another level. One way to get to know people is to travel with them. It's not about having a great idea and a wonderful itinerary and then expecting the beautiful idea will manifest into a magnificent experience. This was a huge awakening for me. Travel for me had always been for pleasure, on my terms and with the co-travellers I chose.

It was always with effortless ease.

These two events were Paul's work-life. I was being introduced to them and he was excited to share them with me, yet, somehow, we were both caught unawares.

What blindsided Paul most was that in all the years that he had worked and travelled with the rally folk and expedition posse, he never expected any fallout where he was involved. He knew them all to be challenging individuals in various other scenarios. This was an eye-opener to say the least.

What was difficult for me was being so far away from home that I felt hostage to these situations. I could not escape them without causing a scene. I could not embarrass Paul on his turf. I was astounded and disappointed that something I was looking forward to, and eager to experience, could go so horribly wrong.

The biggest realisation in the midst of this situation, was that I was back facing one of these characters AGAIN. A narcissistic bully. I knew this was the opportunity that presented itself to reinforce the lessons I needed to learn about bullying: to not suppress my voice and hold back my truth. Just because they were clients or colleagues did not mean I had to capitulate. They were not exempt from being respectful. The Disease to Please was going to be cured.

These two episodes were like my journey through a fire (as clay is fired to become porcelain) to learn that my value is worth more than they could ever pay me to tolerate their rudeness and disrespect. Most importantly I learnt that my Self-Worth comes from Self-Respect, which comes from Self, not from someone else giving it to you. Self-Integrity was the loudest lesson.

The adventures continue and the lessons follow on their trails, as my life and Paul's unfold, with new challenges, new experiences, different people and some of the people we have known for years. It's not about them or the experiences, it's about the choices I make in response to what is happening around me. It's not about getting it right – it's about getting better with each occurrence.

As I continue with my quest to grow and expand into all of who I am here to be, by living my truth, my lessons shared in this book hold me accountable. I ask myself daily, am I better than I was yesterday, what did I learn, what am I grateful for and how can I be better tomorrow?

THE RUBBER HITS THE ROAD – LESSONS LEARNT!

For the first 50 years of my life, I had developed unconscious self-sabotaging mind-sets and behaviours that held me hostage to the pain of my past and I kept repeating the cycle.

In Dr Joe Dispenza's words, "If you want to change your life – you need to look at your life!"

This chapter is a summary of the lessons I learnt through the struggles in my life. It is more about what I needed to learn, rather than about the protagonists or teachers who were the catalysts for my evolution and enlightenment.

It's been liberating to learn how to change my life by changing my mind.

This simple summary will then lead you to the solutions I offer you, the answers that helped me overcome myself and the self-sabotaging mind-sets and behaviours that I had cultivated unconsciously for most of my life.

1. Don't take things personally – take responsibility

I have come to realise that the toughest lessons in life come through the people we love the most and there are sometimes hard facts to digest. It's an illusion to think that they won't hurt our hearts in some way or another. The immediate reflex when there is a disappointment or hurt, is to take it personally as if it was directly intended to cause pain. I started to understand things differently after reading an invaluable book called The Four Agreements by Don Miguel Ruiz.

This small, powerful book of universal principles really helped me, as it also offers real-life application.

One of the four agreements says, "Don't take things personally – people do things because of who THEY are, not because of who you are."

By applying this principle, I realised that people don't

deliberately set out to hurt the person they love. I no longer needed to take responsibility for everything that happened in my life. Instead of blaming others or myself for causing my pain, I could rather choose my response to it, rather than react to their behaviour.

What was alarming for me was the discovery through the studies of significant neuroscientists that 95% of all our behaviours are unconscious, the good ones and the bad ones. The real eye-opener was that many of these behaviours are learned and ingrained and become habits over years.

The result is that we play out these unhealthy habits/patterns. They become reflex actions without thought or consideration, often having harmful effects on others and repercussions for ourselves. Most often, we are unaware of these automatic unconscious behaviours unless they are brought to our attention.

Worst of all, if some of these habits have not been constructively brought to our attention, they can cost us our relationships. Hence they are often self-sabotaging, as well as harmful to others.

The big lesson here is the art of giving constructive feedback and being able to receive it non-defensively. The benefit of raising awareness of unconscious behaviour is that it also provides the opportunity to offer an alternative approach.

A useful Japanese philosophy that defined this beautifully for me is:

Preserve your dignity during tough times. Show emotional maturity and self-control, even when faced with challenges. Remember to be patient, resilient, understanding and compassionate (Gaman).

2. Manage your expectations – we can't control others' actions, only our choices

One of the biggest revelations for me was how we impose our expectations on others without making them aware of them. When these imposed expectations are not met, we make them the cause of our pain, suffering, disappointment, frustration or resentment.

This is what makes any relationship stressful; you are always waiting for someone else to change or do better, so you can be happy. This takes away any responsibility and the control you have over your own actions and life. It is disempowering.

Taking ownership of my own agency was a game-changer. Making my own decisions as to what am I going to do about any situation is far more empowering than imposing my need for others to change their behaviour, to make it alright for me. I realised that there was self-inflicted pain in wanting and waiting for someone else to change, rather than changing my point of view. It was far easier to manage the expectations I had placed on them, and rather choose how I deal with the circumstances in which I found myself.

The only locus of control we have is over our own thoughts, words, actions and behaviour. Even in one family, we cannot impose expectations on everybody, because although we all live under one roof, we will not hold the same set of values and treat each other the same way.

This lesson for me was highlighted in one of the Japanese philosophies on life:

Shikita ga nai: Let go of what you cannot change. Recognise that there are some things just out of our control and that's okay. Let go and focus on what you can change.

3. Every relationship is co-created – it's not just about the other person

With the understanding that every relationship is co-created, both positively and negatively, it really doesn't matter who sets the ball in motion. More important is who is prepared to drop their ego and look at the bigger picture.

For many years I would play the name, blame and shame game. The result was that the essence of whatever conflict I was dealing with would be derailed and become a power struggle of right and wrong and the focus of the debate was lost.

My lesson was to shift perspective from blame and accusation to "what is this teaching me" or "how do I become a better person through this, so I can move forward having grown from the experience?"

4. Creating holistic changes – body, mind, spirit

I was in pursuit of well-being in body, mind and spirit. I also had to consider what would bring me true happiness and inner peace. The biggest test in living the changes I wanted, was not to be swayed or deterred by my environment or because I was in a new relationship and, as a result, slip back into the Disease to Please.

Creating the changes was vital not only because they were damaging to me emotionally, but because of the ripple effects on my body, for which I had already paid the price enough through my previous illnesses. This was also one of my biggest motivators. My cancer episodes were clearly the outer manifestation of deep-seated, unresolved hurt that was stuck in my body whether in cellular memory or energy blockages.

Healthy food and good supplementation were not going to be the silver bullet. Overall well-being was a priority for me. I needed to be more holistic and balanced in all areas of my life by living more mindfully. I could no longer allow myself to fall back to where I had come from. I was given a wake-up call for a reason and I owed it to myself to take responsibility for the choices I made, regardless of who was, or wasn't, in my life. Nobody can save me from me, except me.

I discovered a number of age-old philosophies and traditions from cultures around the world where people are consciously practising living a well life. They have formed the bedrock on which I base the way I live my life. Some of them are: the timeless wisdom of Hygge in Denmark – to get away from the rat race to relax and enjoy life's quieter pleasures with or without others; the spirit of Ubuntu (humanity) in South Africa; Lagom in Sweden – a philosophy that aims for balance in every aspect of life; Wabi Sabi (acceptance of transience and imperfection) and Kaizen (change for the better or continual improvement) in Japan, and the teachings of Buddhism. They are applicable to us all, offering a way of living life with simple principles that keep us conscious and accountable for our choices.

5. Remain true to me in all relationships

As much as my relationship with Paul is my dream come true, I was a little nervous as to how I would navigate the challenges that might arise between us. I knew that the true test of how well I had learnt my life lessons in relationships, was going to be on the journey through life with Paul. However, what I also believed was that we were in each other's lives at the right time for the right reason. We were gifted to each other to grow and we would be the best teachers and healers for each other without burdening each other with that responsibility.

It was an eye-opener to shift perspective and view the "teacher" (positive and negative ones) with appreciation for what they taught me about myself, rather than see them as the villains in the saga. In fact they have shown me what I may not otherwise have seen or may have rejected.

It was important to go into this relationship with a different mind-set of owning all of who I am, the shiny bits and the shady bits, and to lay it all out as things arose and not hide or pretty things up. The truth, the whole truth and nothing but the truth.

I was open and honest with Paul from the get go about who I am and what's important to me. We discussed the non-negotiables and learnt to articulate with love, respect and confidence, rather than fear it would raise conflict or risk the relationship. I made peace with the fact that if he didn't like what I shared early on, I had a choice to make. It was important to me to share my fears, vulnerabilities, and where I had gone wrong in relationships, and not to create a skewed perception that because I worked in the world of personal development, I have it all together. No! I am still a student of life and a work in progress.

I had to keep reminding myself of my two Achilles heels and areas for improvement:

- Fearing to speak my truth for fear of repercussion i.e. loss of love or loss of the relationship. My lesson was to fear even more the repercussion of not speaking, and its potential cost to me.
- To prioritise me, which includes maintaining healthy boundaries. The important part was not to lose myself in the relationship in order to guarantee continued love and fall back into the Disease to Please.

The interesting thing about the second one, is that neither Paul nor I was good at prioritising ourselves, because we are naturally more "givers" than "receivers". Where it became challenging was when I was observing in Paul, the very thing that I had done, and that in itself can be a gift or a curse. It can be an obstacle in the relationship or an opportunity to support each other to shift without judgement or criticism. It is also tough for a giver to hear you say "you have to top up your tank before topping up others". Although giving is a noble quality, it leaves you depleted if it's not managed in balance.

All I can say to you dear seekers of change – it's not comfortable, it's not easy and at times you may even say, "Why does this have to be so hard" and my answer is going to be in the words of: Robin Sharma: "Change is difficult in the beginning; messy in the middle and glorious in the end."

My word of encouragement when you are going through the difficult and messy part is to think about the pain of staying where you have come from, and whether that is where you want to be for the rest of your life. So what is your alternative? The choice is always yours.

As humans we will always default to pain avoidance, whether it is physical or emotional. Just remember, you will be in pain if you stay – guaranteed. You have been there before and you will just be recycling. The other option is to go through the pain of changing, which guarantees you something else, even though you don't know what that looks like. This, by the laws of life, has to be different from what you have known, and is going to bring another result. It's a chance worth taking, isn't it?

The most important and rewarding part of my growth was honouring my truth. I got to respect myself and be more at peace with me because my life was more congruent and authentic. I wasn't feeling one thing (that was true for me) and doing something else (to please someone else) resulting in restlessness and brewing resentment inside me. The clincher for me was the realisation that my incongruence was living a life that was dishonest to me and others. The nett result of that endeavour was clearly not a happy ending.

The biggest cause of stress in my life was living an inauthentic and incongruent life. What others thought or wanted was more important in my quest for love and acceptance. The fact that I allowed my life to be determined by others' needs and wants or to be at the mercy of how others treated me because I didn't stand up for myself, was a travesty. The tragedy is how dependent I became on others' behaviour towards me - a recipe for disaster and misery. The main result was distress, which resulted in dis-ease that ended up in disease and, luckily not, death. Others are not so fortunate.

My biggest lesson in taking care of my well-being is being present and conscious about who and what I include in my life – because I bear the consequences of my choices. So I ask myself these check-in questions:

- Am I being true to myself?
- Does it/they add value or not?
- What can I learn?
- Am I doing it to please them or appease them?

CONCLUSION

I think the hardest part about doing any inner work, is awareness, understanding and then acceptance that who you are has an element of genetics to it. History certainly affects you. However, epigenetics (the study of how your behaviours and environment can cause changes that affect the way your genes work), has proved you have the power to change what you may have inherited. You don't have to buy into it and accept it as your lot in life.

Who you are is reflected around you by the experiences that you have gone through and the people you encounter who have in some way positively or negatively affected your life. When you change your view about it all, everything else around you changes. Life doesn't happen to you – it happens for you. Even in the horrific traumas that thousands of people have faced beyond their control, they still have a choice of whether they will be victims or victors. So many people have turned trauma into triumph.

There's an old story about two boys who were raised by an alcoholic father. They grew up and one son became an alcoholic. When someone asked him what had happened after all his years of watching the way his father's life went, he said, "What choice do I have? My father is an alcoholic." The other son never touched a drop of alcohol. When the stranger asked him why he never drank, he said, "How could I? Look what it did to my father."

The bottom line is that we all have a choice and the perspective you choose will determine your future. What excites me about this life I have lived is that I have broken the female familial pattern of The Disease to Please.

I am so grateful to all my teachers – I AM because of ALL OF THEM!

Where did my mother fit into this new phase of personal growth? I never heard from her again except for one email about a year after she exited. It read: "I have some information on your husband that I would want to know if I was you. Let me know when you want to meet."

I knew in my belly this was not going to be good news and was definitely not going to be, "Jo, life's too short. Let's get together and chat about what happened and find a way to work things, so we can at least continue our relationship."

I sat with her email for a good few days, all the while tuning into my gut and my heart. In my mind, I still wanted to think it could be a positive opportunity to reconnect and move forward. Yet the knot in my stomach told me otherwise. And so I arrived at the conclusion that this was not going to be any different from any other time when my mother was going to deliver a message of doom. This was not going to be a reunion meeting and "let's put the past behind us and move on". I could not let my eternal optimism have any more false hope. If my mom had any intentions of a constructive and healing conversation, she would have connected long before this and it would not be shrouded by a message that sounded more like she was about to pass down sentence.

I could not bring myself to sit at the same table knowing she was not there about me and us healing and building. She would be in her power play where she gets to be the presiding magistrate delivering judgement. Where would that leave us? Still without a mom and daughter bridge. I was not prepared to take the chance only to end up being angry with myself for not listening to my gut and allowing myself to go down that dead-end road again.

I never replied. It was taking enough of my strength and resolve to face the hell of my then fast-degenerating marriage to have to face my mother and her disparaging lectures. Even if it was important information, I was not giving her the satisfaction of bringing further doom and gloom into my life.

That was December 2014 and I left my husband a year

later. I sent a message to her via her lifelong "anchor friend" John, that I was divorced. I never heard a word. I don't know why I even expected some sort of acknowledgement.

On 21 June 2021, my mother's 80th birthday, Paul and I spoke about acknowledging her in some way, as it was a day to honour. So I sent her a beautiful bowl of her favourite flowers anonymously with a note, "Wishing you a wonderful celebration of 80 years and all you have accomplished. Thank you for the beautiful memories and all that I have learnt from you."

I wanted to acknowledge my mom in some way but without any need or expectation of a response. I did not want to open any doors. I was at peace with the way things were and wanted to keep my life undisturbed.

Ironically when I gave the name and address to the florist, she spontaneously said, "Oh, Mrs Forbes, I know her well."

"I would appreciate your keeping this anonymous please."

Upon reflection her response was, "She is a very difficult lady."

I was silently sad – what a way to be remembered.

A year later, the day before my mother's 81st birthday I received a call. "Hi Jo, it's Claire."

She was the last person I expected to hear from as all my mother's friends had also severed ties with me years before, for whatever reason. They were forced to make a choice based on the story my mother told them about her awful daughter.

"Hi Claire," I said tentatively, not expecting what I was about to hear.

"I know it's been many years since we last spoke, and this is a very difficult call but I felt you needed to know. Eunice has passed away."

It was all over. My mom was no longer someone I spoke of who was alive, but our relationship was dead.

"What happened?"

"I found her lying dead on her bathroom floor this morning. She must have had a heart attack while she was on the loo."

My body went ice cold and my heart sank. There was a loud silence till I responded, "She always feared she would die alone, and she even said to me once: 'Who will find me lying dead on my bathroom floor one day?'"

"Jo," Claire went on, "your mom was very difficult and it got worse, so we distanced ourselves from her a couple of years ago, although I still managed the garden for her. Today was my gardening day and she didn't answer the door or her phone."

My heart broke for the soul who had died alone in the world on a cold winter's night, riddled with pain that the world experienced as anger. Yet I was relieved that her inner suffering was over and her soul could rest.

"Claire, I am sorry for the difficulties you endured that led you and Gray to become estranged from my mother. It couldn't have been easy."

"Jo, we all knew your mom and what really happened between you and her. We watched it over the years and we dared not get involved. We could not even mention your name or she would cut the conversation. She gave us all ultimatums: if we stayed in contact with you she would write us off. Sadly we all fell for it and we, too, are sorry ..."

Hearing these words from Claire after all these years left me feeling vindicated and relieved. I always wondered what distorted version my mother shared with her friends about why she and I were no longer connected. However, the truth is always the truth and it does reveal itself in the passage of time.

I thanked her and said goodbye. It was a shock for all of us for different reasons and needed digesting.

Although I had lost my mom years before, you can never be prepared for the experience of death no matter what the relationship. She was still my mom and this time it was final. She exited my life seven years prior without a word, not even a warning. We never got to say goodbye.

The only choice available to me now was how I would resolve this within myself and choose to remember my mom.

So I went to the beach that night, lit a candle and spoke to her soul with love, compassion, understanding and gratitude that have come to me with my maturity and wisdom. The next day on her 81st birthday, 21 June 2022, I honoured the life of an incredible woman, by writing a poem and reading it to Mother Ocean.

So I seal this memoir with a message and a wish for you, my readers. Live your truth fearlessly – regret free. Honour your values; respect who you are and make conscious choices that you can live with.

Dr David Molapo: "Your attitude determines your altitude."

PART 5

The gateway to your guiding star – your truest version

Seven simple steps to creating your winning formula
– to take you from wounded to worthy and wise!

THE GATEWAY TO YOUR GUIDING STAR – YOUR TRUEST VERSION

The first question to ask yourself before entering the Gate to your Guiding Star is:

"Who am I?" How easy is that to answer? It can be daunting because we wear many different hats that we think define us, given the varied roles we play throughout our lives. Mother, daughter, sister, friend, colleague, CEO and so much more. So who are we? How do we reconcile all these parts of us and be congruent with our essence? It can feel confusing, overwhelming and even unsettling. We can even feel lost or disconnected from ourselves by trying to fit in or accommodate others' requirements or expectations. This is where the rot sets in for the Disease to Please to permeate into all the areas of our lives.

Our human understanding is that the different roles we play are our identity and give us a sense of purpose and value. What is astounding is the realisation that we are not what we do i.e. the roles we fulfil. We are beings of light that shine on this playground called life.

If you can accept who you are and just be you, without fear of rejection or repercussions, you'll no longer need to play roles. It is courageous to allow people to see all of who you are. It may even feel vulnerable, but the only one who needs to co-exist with all our parts and make peace with that, is you. Your vibe will attract your tribe.

Your question may be, "Where do I start and how?"

I will now take you through Seven Simple Steps that will change your life!

Seven simple steps to creating your winning formula – to take you from wounded to worthy and wise!

Here is an opportunity for you to shift gear in your life

and take a leap of faith to explore some tried-and-tested tools that will help you move towards the direction of your dreams.

Get yourself a brand-new journal that becomes your reflection space where you can craft how you are going to reshape the way you live your life and commit to the choices that will uphold them. Let your journal become your reminder of your commitments to your life that YOU are choosing for YOU! Your journal also becomes your accountability partner. Let's open your journal now and start with a promise to yourself.

What is the promise you are committing to for your best and truest life?

Remember, this is time you are giving to yourself, to take ownership of your life, letting go of the name, blame, shame, guilt, remorse and regrets of what has passed. The time for you is NOW. Life is not a dress rehearsal. I invite you to start your journey by reflecting and answering the questions that follow.

I will open each of the seven stages with:

- A brief explanation of what each stage means;
- An inspiring example or case study that I witnessed; in a number of my clients – these are just a few of many;
- A task that will either be a reflection or an activity; and
- Some truisms to anchor the learning.

I know most of us are not crazy about change. Our natural impulse is to come up with all sorts of reasons (excuses mostly), why we should stay right where we are and keep everything the same – even if we're miserable or in pain. The voices in your head try to make a case that change is impossible and why you shouldn't or can't do it. I bet you can hear those voices even as you read this. When you make a change in your life, those voices get louder and feed the fear monster inside that holds you back. It is, in fact, just the ego mind testing you, needing to maintain the status quo and stay in control, because when you change the paradigm, it loses its power. This is actually a good thing. A note to self is that ego has its place when we need to survive a situation. However, it must not control us, as it can hold us back from being the best version of ourselves and living our best life.

Remember: your fear is a retreat from life. It is False Evidence Appearing Real. It prevents you from experiencing as much joy, fulfilment, satisfaction and growth as you can.

Whenever I feel stuck, I remind myself of the Decision, Vision and Actions (DVA) to which I committed. And while you may never be able to silence those voices, this simple acronym can help you turn their volume down so you can focus your attention on what will serve you. Every time you act in spite of your fearsome voices, your soul's voice grows stronger.

This is only the beginning of the process – it is a journey not a destination. Your doubts and fears will continue to arise but stick with me and I'll hold your hand as we walk gently together. Step-by-step we will move forward, towards the moment when you can take action to make powerful, positive, lasting change in your life, with courage and confidence

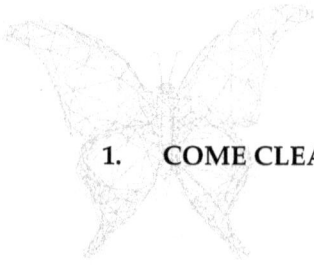

1. COME CLEAN WITH YOURSELF

When we are in pain, it is difficult to acknowledge that many of the circumstances that caused the pain are co-created and that we have an equal part to play in it appearing in our lives. So we often seek a protagonist in the situation to blame and deflect from ourselves. This, in some way, seems to free us from any responsibility or part we played in it, so we can handle the pain better. However, when we find ourselves stuck in the same recurring cycle or pattern e.g. encountering the same kind of people who hurt us or the same kind of heart-breaking relationships, we need to step back and begin by asking ourselves "who is the common factor?"

Come clean with yourself means: stop the name, blame and shame game and take responsibility for YOUR choices. This is where you start to break the patterns of the past and you have the opportunity to craft new ones that serve you better and ultimately bring you more of what you want.

A. Client Story: Veronica

Veronica was a 40-year-old mother of two, married to a difficult, controlling man who was the craftiest fraud. She was a loving, caring and kind mom, friend and daughter and had her own business. Money was thin because her husband was always a "big-ideas and big-spender guy" and loved living the high life far beyond his means. He was great at being creative and coming up with yet another story and another excuse about his business, the deals and the financial difficulties they were facing, in the hope it would placate Veronica.

However, he was running out of hogwash and the screws were tightening on them financially, which inevitably put strain on the relationship. The tensions were riding high, his anger and frustration were quick to flare. The children were rattled and unsettled and Veronica was desperate to keep it all together. Still, she had her family to consider and the shame of exposing it was unthinkable.

The reality is that the writing had been on the wall for a number of years. There were many signposts showing her this was a lonely road to hell. Though she no longer fully trusted him, she would try to make excuses.

Veronica considered what her options were – stay like this and it would predictably get worse (past behaviour is the best predictor of the future) or face the reality and make a difficult change now, which would yield different results and a brighter future. She responded in despair, with wide-open, frightened, sunken eyes.

"Jo how will I deal with all the responsibilities and the mess we are in. We have the children and family? How do we break this up? What will happen to us all? What about the kids? How will we manage financially? He will be so angry, as everything these days is confrontational. We can't even have a normal conversation. I am walking on eggshells, to avoid any conflict. I can't bear his anger. Divorce is so messy and the thought of moving out is a nightmare.

"Where will I go and what about the kids and their school? And Christmas is coming up, it's not a good time for everybody." She was so depleted from worry and anxiety from all she was holding inside her that she dissolved into tears.

This is common to many of us. It's difficult to face the reality of a painful and destructive situation that we have allowed to spiral into a dark hole of desperation, hurt and fear.

My next question to her was: "Veronica what is the mental and emotional cost to you and your kids for the stability you all need in your lives? How sustainable is this? With what you know, are you prepared to wait until something even worse happens? How is your health being affected by this? Are you prepared to live the next 40 years of your life like this … because you might not make it?"

She was so overwhelmed at the enormity of facing this as her future life. She sobbed helplessly, and said, "What do I do? Where to from here?"

My response was simple: "What does your HEART say – not your head?"

She said, "To get out"

"Ok, what does your gut say?"

Immediately she said with vehemence in her voice, "Get out!"

I followed on by saying, "So if you follow the 'The Committee' in your head that suggests otherwise, how do your heart and gut feel?"

On reflection, she said, "Get out."

My final question was: "If your bestie was in this situation what would you say?"

Again, she said, "Get out while you can, before it's too late."

I warmly responded, "Therefore, with this resounding conclusion, what is your next step?"

She looked at me like a frightened deer caught in the headlights and I took her hand, "The biggest hurdle is making the decision. Then we sit together and figure out a plan – step-by-step. You have found help and support here and you have your mom and beloved friends behind you. Yes, you have to do the hard yards yourself but you are not alone ..."

I continued encouraging her. "Eventually, like everything in life, this too shall pass and like everything that you have overcome in your life, you will overcome this, too, with more confidence and restored self-worth. This is the example you want to be for your children. What their dad does will teach them about what is and is not acceptable in life. Your children will model themselves on how you live your life and the choices you make will impact their world view. So, showing courage to stand for your values and what is true and right for you, is an important life principle for your girls to learn and you will be their best teacher and role model. In the long run what you are learning now may prevent the girls from going down a similar path later in their lives."

That was the day Veronica took the first step towards a better life. Today she is remarried to a wonderful man who loves, appreciates and supports her and her children

B.   *Reflections to help you come clean with yourself*

    a.   Think of a few changes you would like to make and the fears holding you back. List them in your journal. Today I would like to make this change ...

But I am afraid that ...

How will you feel once you have made one or more of these changes?

b. There are stories we tell ourselves that we believe to be true, that hijack us from taking a step towards the life of our dreams. These "what-ifs" are the reasons that "justify" why we cannot move toward change. To counteract these stories, we need to separate fact from fiction so we can make clear choices based on TRUTH! So write them down ...

The story I tell myself is ...

The meaning I give the story about me is ...

The truth is ...

This will happen if I stay stuck in my story ... and the cost to me will be ...

This will happen when I move towards possibility and opportunity...

c. Let's look at what you say YES to when you really want to say NO!

I would like to say NO to ...

How will I feel once I have said NO to one or more of these?

But I am afraid that ...

d. Allow yourself to throw an "I don't want to jump!" tantrum by doing an excuse inventory. Write down all the obstacles still in your way. These could be your own feelings, the feelings of others, physical logistics, practicalities etc. Exhaust all of the reasons your mind tells you that you can't and shouldn't take a giant leap into the future you deeply desire.

e. If resistance was a person, what would it look like? Give them a name and describe them below. When you have a clear vision of your resistance, kindly say out loud to them "I acknowledge you, but I'm going to keep moving forward anyway."

f. Harness your fear and let it fuel you.

"I embrace my fear of …
And release it to create space for change."
How do you feel now after your reflections and the insights you have gained?
The truth doesn't hold you hostage – it's only the repression of your mind that does. This is what I believe is meant by "The truth will set you free".

C.   *Truisms to remind you:*
- Honesty starts with self about self.
- You attract who you are.
- If you want to change your life start by looking at your life.
- Perception is personal.
- Pain drives change.
- Anger is a signal to pay attention and do something different.
- Guilt is a ghost that seeks entertainment and takes you down a road to nowhere except torment.
- No one is here to fix your life – the victim to victor journey is an inside-out job.
- Staying stuck in the Drama Triangle prevents you from taking responsibility.
- You need to go through this. It's an important part of your self-worth growth path. If you don't know what you don't want, how do you find what you do want?
- Misery seeks company – what company are you choosing?
- Finding your voice – speaking your truth.
- Lessons are blessings – they are experiences that teach you what you need to learn.
- Disease to Please is when your value is determined by others' approval. You will never find peace. You will always be striving. This will leave you unsure of who you are and doubt/question your true value.

"True freedom is when your thoughts, feelings and actions are flying in formation with what is true and honouring of you – no matter the personal price." JM

2. DESIGN YOUR DREAM LIFE – CREATE YOUR OWN DREAM BOARD

We acknowledge that change can be hard. However, the advantage of going through those difficult times is that it clarifies and informs us of what we don't want. One of the biggest things that holds us back from going after the life we want, is our perception of change and the lack of confidence in ourselves that we can do it. We envision the worst will happen instead of what is possible. We think of change as an uninvited guest who sweeps our house of the most valuable things. Fear creeps in – fear of repercussions whether it be loss of some kind or fear of failure. Instead of imagining the ways that we might feel satisfied, fulfilled or enriched, we imagine all we might lose and or have to give up.

While change may bring some loss, it's often loss of the old self and an opportunity to step into a more authentic life. It's about being discerning about whom we invite into our lives; where we feel good about who we are and how we choose to live. Every end brings a beginning with it – it's the cycle of life and can be a source of comfort through your transition. It's time to begin imagining your most meaningful life and how it can invite a flood of abundance, joy, well-being and purpose.

"Build your own dreams before someone uses you to build theirs." JM

A.   Client Story: Suzette
I was always in awe of my friend, Suzette, who is now 83. She is a fine example of manifestation. Suzette is quietly strong, elegant and a gracious lady, simply and beautifully groomed and has consciously created the life she has, on so many levels. Suzette has been creating her dream board for her life for more than 40 years. She has been

consistent and committed in her approach by applying the simple tools and techniques founded in an ancient concept which has been embedded in universal laws, more commonly known as the law of attraction.

Suzette manifested her current 35-year marriage to a man who has the qualities she intended. She manifested her spiritual growth path; her life and lifestyle as it is today and her dream boards have evolved through her journey of life.

When I asked her how she "fuelled them" or "breathed life" into them she said. "You visualise it as if it has already happened. Feel what it feels like to already be where you want to be and have what it is you are manifesting. Immerse yourself in a sensory experience and feel it deeply and daily. Then let it go and carry on with your day till the next day and repeat this ritual. It's like posting your intentions to the Universe and leaving the details "of how it will come into being" up to them. You never go to a restaurant and place your order, then go to the chef and tell him how to prepare your meal, do you? So you focus on 'the what' and the Universe takes care of 'the how'. Then trust the process."

How it unfolds is not your job – that's the Universe's job because our minds are limited. When we get into brainiac mode, we complicate things by overthinking and overanalysing. We can miss out on something even better than we could have imagined when we ring-fence our ideas into boxes of limitations formed in our minds.

Although the unknown may seem uncertain, daunting and sometimes even scary, in fact that is where endless possibility resides. So, dare to dream and imagine, let it go and be surprised and delighted by how it all unfolds. It will do so in ways you may never have been able to imagine.

B. *Activity to design your dream life*

Time to go within and imagine. Take some time out. Don't wait for it to become available – it never will. There will always be something pulling at your responsibility string.

a) Find a quiet, blissful space that is your happy place where you can just be with yourself – somewhere you can tap into your deepest desires. Let it be a place free of distractions and devices – indoors or outdoors Light a candle, burn incense, do whatever feels comforting, comfortable and beautiful to you.

b) Take in five to 10 deep breaths and slowly let them out through your nose. It slows your mind and body down and will help you settle into yourself. Feel your body's own rhythm and hear your heart's calling.

c) Be open to what unfolds, without limitation or hesitation. This IS YOUR time for YOU to meet you, where it's quiet and free of all distractions and the "committee" is off duty, where you can sit and JUST BE, – be with yourself, so you can delve into your deepest desires. Allow yourself to free fall into the expansion of your imagination and allow your musings to flow. Invite your heart's lifelong yearnings into your awareness. See it, hear it, feel it (don't think it), so you can start to paint the picture of your dream Life.

d) Remain in the present moment. Avoid drifting into the past (it's gone) or the future (it's unknown) Possibility is in the present moment – a blank canvas to imagine yourself into your desired future.

e) Be clear, be specific and describe in microscopic detail. WRITE DOWN THE FIRST THINGS THAT COMES TO MIND – NO SECOND GUESSING or DOUBTING... just let it all flow out of your heart, into your hand and onto the page in your journal.

Here is a fun way to get the ball rolling if you have hit a blank ... it's called: "The Story of My Life"

a) You have just been given a contract to write your autobiography with a major publishing company. Your agent, Demanding Daniel, is putting you under pressure to get to press. He has decided to get you started with a few probing questions.

b) First take a piece of A4 paper. Fold it in half and then half again.

c) Choose the title of your favourite song as the title of your book. Write the title on the front cover.

d) On the inside cover (page 2) list the table of contents:
   - What accomplishment are you most proud of?
   - For what would you like to be remembered?
   - If you knew you couldn't fail, what would you do?

e) On page 3 draw a picture of something that is important to you.

f) On the back cover of the book, draw a picture reflecting how you are feeling today about your journey.

Points to consider as you zoom into your envisioning:
   ☆ How you spend your time.
   ☆ Whom you're spending it with.
   ☆ What you're doing.
   ☆ How you bring in fun.
   ☆ What sparks your curiosity and creativity?
   ☆ What brings you closer to feeling connected to yourself?

To form this vision, ask yourself these questions:
- How would I like to feel on a daily basis?
- What do I need to be happy, satisfied and fulfilled with who I am?
- What value will going after my dreams add to my personal growth?
- How does my work fit into my personal life?
- How does fun fit into my personal life?
- Where does money fit into my life and what will it bring me?
- How do I envision my health?

Make notes about your vision so you remember it. You may even want to capture it on a vision or dream board or digital collage of words and images, and connect with it daily.

To move closer to your vision, connect with the following:
- What are the choices and actions I've made that have led me away from my vision? Examples:
  - I've stuck in a job I hate for 10 years and haven't looked to develop the skills that will help me leave for something better.
  - I've stuck in an unhappy and unfulfilling relationship for so long that I have not empowered myself so I can leave with confidence.
- What new choices and actions will support me in making my vision a reality? What are the positive possibilities?
- What do I need to know or believe to bring my vision to fruition?
- Which new choice(s) or action(s) will I integrate this week?

C. *Truism as a reminder to:*
- Spend time daily connecting with the possibilities and opportunities of manifesting your dreams – like watering your garden. Why waste water on weeds that are your fears? Embrace all that unfolds as a gift.
- Take or make the time to create your life – no one can do that for you. Treat it like an investment – what you put in is what you will get out.
- Live by choice rather than by chance.
- YOU and only you have the master key to your life.

3.   PRIORITISE YOU – PUT YOUR OXYGEN MASK ON FIRST

"How?" you might ask. When you're going after what you want, it's not unusual to put your own life's vision behind someone else's – your partner's, your family's – especially if their vision might seem more financially lucrative, or if they've already invested the time and energy that you haven't.

You might even have been taught that it's noble to go with the flow and be the support, not selfish, so you let go of having any vision of your own. The truth is, most of us would never want to be called selfish because we think it is unacceptable. The world's perception of selfish is taking care of ourselves to the exclusion of others. The result is you become either a martyr, victim or doormat and none of these is heroic or rewarding.

If you're like me, you were taught or believe that it's bad to be selfish. So to put yourself first or just making yourself a priority, is unthinkable.

If you have the Disease to Please and your self-worth is measured by others' approval, selfish has such a negative connotation. Most people-pleasers swing to the opposite end of the spectrum and overcompensate to become selfless so they are seen as caring and considerate.

We're almost never taught that being selfish might mean you also consider your needs, and your needs matter as much as everyone else's, which ultimately allows you to be more present and available to help others.

I have so many examples of this. It is like a pandemic that occurs in families and marriages, and is the ultimate recipe for disaster.

A. Client Story: Tarzan Tom and Joyful Jane

To protect confidentiality, I will light-heartedly and respectfully call this couple Tarzan Tom and Joyful Jane. They were in their 40s with two teenage children, living a contented life in suburbia, driving comfortable cars and navigating a full, busy life. Tom was a corporate high flyer, super successful, well respected among his peers and highly regarded by his clients. His drive to serve and succeed became a self-perpetuating cycle. The harder he worked, the more he achieved, the more he did, the more accolades he received, the more money he earned, the more he could comfortably provide for his family.

On the flip side, the family he supported never saw him. He was either working late or travelling for the business.. When they did get together, he was like a guest in their house. Meals at the table were pragmatic, superficial updates without heartfelt connection or deep, meaningful conversation, let alone laughter. As much as the kids cared for their dad, neither really knew him and he was out of touch with their day-to-day lives. Kids, being who they are, accepted this as normal and got on with their lives. Routinely, after dinner every evening, Dad would leave the table and go back to his desk till long after everyone went to bed.

Jane, in the meantime, was being mom, homemaker and wife. Her day job was also demanding in the corporate world, albeit to a lesser degree. So at the end of each day, after fulfilling all these roles to her 100% best, she was exhausted. She had no energy or capacity, and no time to do anything for herself.

The worst part of all was that Tom and Jane became functional co-habitants as a result of their lifestyle choices. They had no real connection because they had expended their energy and time on everything and everyone else outside of their relationship. It was no surprise at all that their lack of prioritising themselves and their relationship would end up in a fractured family and hollow marriage.

When they came to me with their relationship in tatters, Tom asked me, completely bewildered:

"How did we get here when we are both working so hard and giving our all … where did it all go wrong?"

Jane interjected with a despairing sigh and said, "But Tom, you don't stop working or switch off your devices. Then you fall into bed exhausted every night and there is nothing left for me and the kids."

To which he retorted, *"But I do it for all of you. You are always busy with the kids and fall into bed exhausted, too."*

She shot back at him with, *"Well, I have to do it all because you are never around to help."*

These conversations often spiral into combat and are neither helpful nor healthy – a perfect example of the blame game. The bottom line is there was an imbalance in priorities between emotional and practical needs. Both parties were in pain as their emotional needs had been neglected due to the over performance on the practicalities of life. It brought loss of connection, loss of self and loss of relationship and potentially loss of marriage.

Relationships cannot and should not be taken for granted, even the one with yourself. They require nurturing. Without regular deposits into the emotional bank account, they wither and die from depletion.

Activity to prioritise you

So, now, I invite you to understand and embrace selfish. Put your oxygen mask on first and lose the idea of being selfless. When you are selfless, you matter less – you are not a priority. Others needs matter more. Interestingly this allegedly gallant act of kindness drains energy and is followed by a slow-brewing resentment that eventually bubbles up through our moods and behaviours. We become reactive rather than responsive, which is often evident in verbal spillage like "I give everybody everything and I have nothing left"; "I never have time for me"; "Nobody ever thinks I might need time out"; "Everyone just takes advantage of my kindness". There is simply nothing left of you available to you for you.

As I mentioned before, if you don't take the time, no one will give you that time. Saying you don't have time becomes an excuse. People will take as long as you give. Why should they change? It's working out perfectly for them. We get what we allow.

Let's reflect on the times you've put someone else's needs and wants ahead of your own. What was the payoff? This exploration will help you begin to notice, when you back down without thinking, when you consider your own desires first (or at all). This activity isn't about apportioning blame or judgement, it's to help you identify what you want and how you might be pushing your own needs to the side.

It's also part of **Coming clean with yourself** and taking ownership of your choices.

a) List the significant times you have not voiced your needs and desires because you thought doing so was selfish. Write down the negative beliefs and excuses you have about going after what you want.

b) Looking at this list, write down the consequences you suffered as a result of not speaking your truth. Where did you miss out on what you wanted?

c) Think back to times in your current or last few relationships when you deferred to what your partner wanted, or to what a friend or family member wanted. Let's say you were talking about watching a movie or ordering take-out. Did you wait for them to voice their opinion, and automatically agree? Or maybe you've acquiesced about more important aspects of the relationship such as not discussing your career or business goals because he/she didn't want to, or theirs seemed to be more important? Or perhaps you decided not to voice your objection to someone's behaviour out of the fear of conflict or rejection?

d) Make a list of the most important times you can remember when you didn't ask for what you wanted or times when you put someone else's needs before your own. What were the consequences of not speaking your truth? Did you miss out on getting what you wanted, and did you resent the other person for it? Did that someone else also miss out on getting to know you more fully?

e) How are you currently putting your dreams on hold because you think it might negatively affect your partner, friends or family? Are you telling yourself that you'll find time for your dreams after they find theirs? Do you quietly withhold your dreams, telling yourself that your time has already passed?

f) Often we have an unconscious pattern that has been created where we define our value by giving all we can and people love us for that. If we don't do that, will we lose the love?

g) Each time you hold back on your needs, wants and desires, it leads to consequences that are mostly undesirable. What is one way you can begin to share your dreams and claim what you really want? Make it simple, do-able and something that you'll follow up. The point is to take one small step toward your dreams so you can begin to give them a voice and breathe life into them.

Even if it feels selfish at first, take notice of how you feel when you embrace taking care of yourself. Your answers here will help you become aware of when you are about to put your own needs and wants aside again. Notice these moments in your life and pause. Then begin to gently nudge yourself toward stating what you do want.

B.   *Truisms to consider when PRIORITISING YOU*

- By putting ourselves first, we teach people how to treat us.
- Putting yourself first is necessary, not selfish.
- Being self-centred is selfish.
- Self-worth comes from Self – so you have to value you, before others will value you. That way you build your self-esteem and self-confidence. This is one of the ways that people will respect you.

"Until you value yourself, you won't value your time.
Until you value your time, you will not do anything
worthwhile with it". **M. Scott Peck**

4. REWIRE YOUR THINKING – HOW CANCER CALLED ME TO TAKE OWNERSHIP OF MY LIFE

There are many people from whom I took inspiration to help me change my life by changing my mind. We can create a different future. The choice is always ours, if we are prepared to put in the time and effort. We cannot solve problems with the same mind-set that created them, so what are we going to do about it? Albert Einstein said, "Insanity is doing the same thing over and over again and expecting a different result."

The biggest part of change is not the change itself. It is our mind-set around it. It takes discipline, determination and commitment to whom you want to become as a result of the change. It is an unwavering high-value priority to become a happier and healthier you – as simple as that. Happy heart, peaceful mind, healthy body.

Inevitably in life, "sh*t happens" and our resolve is shaken or tested. Accept it as part of life because that's how we measure our progress. It's not about perfection, it's about progression. Being further along the continuum of change than when the journey started becomes your motivation to continue the work and becomes a self-fulfilling prophecy. It is the process of rewiring your mind from an old pattern that didn't serve you, to cutting new neural pathways that invite the change. It is the persistence and the discipline to keep practising the new steps you are taking so they become a way of life. This requires you also to be the eye in the storm when the winds of life come gusting around us. Remember the payoff of change is higher than the pain of staying the same.

A. *Case studies to show it is possible*

There are an infinite number of examples of people who have overcome huge obstacles, or come from traumatic and disadvantaged backgrounds, and turned their lives around from victim to victor. Albert Einstein didn't speak till he was four and started reading only at seven. Oprah Winfrey had a scarred childhood. Jim Carey was homeless. Richard Branson has dyslexia. Thomas Edison failed 1000 times before creating the lightbulb. Vincent van Gogh sold only one painting in his lifetime. His fame came posthumously. South African rugby captain, Siya Kolisi, who lead the team to two World Cup victories came from a poor, abusive and disadvantaged young life.

Reflection exercise for self-discovery

If you become your authentic self:
- ☆ What would you lose?
- ☆ What would you gain?
- ☆ What is holding you back?
- ☆ What does your heart truly long for?
- ☆ Are YOU getting in your own way with excuses?

B. *Activity to learn to: SAY "YES" INSTEAD OF "NO"*

So often, we automatically say no to new experiences. This immediately shuts the door on opportunities. We don't quite know what those experiences will be like and yet we fear them. Rather than risk getting hurt or feeling uncomfortable, we simply say no. But where's the gift in that?

Years ago, once I had learned to say yes, it opened a world that I had left unexplored. I learned that by saying yes, I could be comfortable with the uncomfortable and experience a depth of joy and liberation I never thought possible. Believing you can say yes to new opportunities in your life opens you to a genuine curiosity that surpasses all fear. The wonder that you can experience in what is possible, that you never imagined, is inspiring and energising.

Take some time to explore the questions below to help you open up to saying yes – and then saying yes again.

a) If you were totally free of fear, what would you do that you didn't do before?

b) Imagine you're looking back at the present version of you from the future. How have you changed by embracing the power of Yes?

   Example: I used to be afraid of taking time away from my responsibilities, and now I seek out opportunities to take "me time" to recharge.

c) Write down three things to which you are ready to say "yes" this week.

   - X
   - Y
   - Z

Saying yes will become addictive. Once you say yes and experience the way it opens you, you'll feel empowered and excited to keep exploring new things each day

d) What are you afraid will happen if you step out and "say yes"?

e) What will you gain by "saying yes"? How will it change your life?

   Formula for mind-set change:

   - Become aware of your destructive or recycled patterns.
   - Be willing to make the change because you know and believe in the value of doing so.
   - Find constructive approaches or tools to enable the change.
   - Consistently apply the tools to develop new neural pathways that will eventually override old patterns and retrain the brain into new behaviours so it becomes a way of life.
   - The key to consistently applying the tools is to live consciously and fully present in each moment of life so you respond to life rather than react to life. Otherwise the unconscious habits will resurface.

One of the red flags with unconscious habits is that under stress, they can surface on reflex when we are thinking about the problem that has triggered us, rather than how we can manage the problem productively. So self-awareness is key to self-management.

A big note to self is even when you're tripped up, it is not the time to beat yourself up because you deviated from your new path, or to give up. It requires your perseverance to become your new habit. It's not a straight, flat road. Life will test you. That's how you get to see your progress. It's less important to entertain your inner critic than to ask, "am I further along my continuum of progress towards who I am becoming than I was when I started?" Invariably the answer is yes.

C. *Truisms to remind you when times are tough, why reshaping your thinking is vital*
   - You get what you focus on.
   - Your mind is like a garden and your thoughts are the seeds you are planting in it. What are you planting and how are you nourishing it, will determine the kind of fruits you harvest.
   - What you think about expands. The more you feed it the bigger it grows, e.g. I said I didn't want breast cancer or be a divorcee and I got both.
   - Use your pain as a propeller to move forward.
   - Your life is the sum of your choices. Choose your thoughts wisely.

"When you change the way you look at things – the things you look at, will change." Dr Wayne Dyer

5.   SET SOLID BOUNDARIES – WITHOUT THEM YOU ARE ON THE ROAD TO NOWHERE

As you will have read in earlier chapters, I landed in desperate situations because I did not apply boundaries. Behaviours that were not right and unacceptable, I excused or tolerated for peace's sake. I allowed things that were clearly wrong to continue, because I was afraid of the repercussions. I didn't have the confidence to speak my truth. When it all got bad enough, it became more destructive. Why did I wait that long? The painful truth is I allowed it to deteriorate for as long as it did because of my fear.

My boundarylessness and hence my Disease to Please started when I was very young as a learnt behaviour (I know that now). I thought or learnt that if I would do or be what others wanted, needed, commanded or demanded and sometimes threatened me to do, all would be well and I would be a good person and liked/loved/approved of and accepted. Most of all I would belong. Thrown into the mix were my lifelong role models – my mom and gran, the Master Pleasers.

A.   Case study: Jo's Disease to Please

Mom raised me with great principles, ethics and guidance to be self-sufficient and independent. Yet I also learnt by her example to keep the peace in turbulent times. I watched how she would do so to appease her volatile husband. She had a difficult life in her relationships as she made bad husband choices. She made it clear to me that to keep the peace in the house we would just need to toe the line. We had a volatile and often violent life with him, which was distressing for us both. So from a young age, I learnt about playing nicely and peacekeeping. Sadly, my grandmother fell prey to the same trap of peacemaker in her marriage to my grandfather. So the die was cast in the female family lineage.

The Disease to Please gained momentum as I grew older. I would more often than not rather suppress than express my feelings as the repercussions or conflict were not worth it and keeping the peace was familiar. Until I was pushed to my edge (which you will recall in Part 2 Chapter 4).

That was the start of learning the value and necessity of boundaries even for people you love, because boundaries prevent things going sideways and so safeguard relationships.

B.   Reflection - *What is a BOUNDARY?*

A boundary is a limit you set to define what you will and will not do, or what you will or will not accept or tolerate from others. It also prevents you from rescuing someone from the consequences of their destructive behaviour that they need to experience in order to grow.

   a.   What are your boundaries that you need to form or have abandoned?

   b.   What are you tolerating that is insufferable or unacceptable?

   c.   What has being boundary less cost you in your life?

   d.   What is it costing you when you do not uphold your boundaries?

   e.   What is your fear in setting boundaries? Is it real or is it your conditioned mind?

   f.   What will serve your highest good and give you the life you really want? Having boundaries or being boundary less?

   g.   Write a "mantra" for the bold boundaries you want to put into place and practise them through repetition. The more you do it the stronger they will get and ultimately build your self-confidence.

C.   *Truisms to remind you to stay on the boundary bus!*

   • Boundaries begin and end with you. How you make them and how you break them are up to you.

   • Remember, even great people and the people you love need boundaries.

   • Boundaries builds respect. You respect you and others respect you. This builds self-worth.

- By not setting boundaries, you abandon your true self. The consequences include squandering this life you've been given by living it on others' terms.
- You are the one crossing your own boundaries by allowing others to violate them.
- You can't change anyone else or force them to uphold your boundaries. You have a choice: the short-term discomfort of setting limits and keeping them, or the long-term pain of allowing your boundaries to be crossed.
- Boundaries are healthy selfishness and will be a game changer in your life.
- Conflict can simply be the illumination of differences. You can maintain relationships even if you agree to disagree but if you compromise your boundaries you compromise the quality of the relationship.
- Becoming a bold boundary-builder means that you care at least as much about your own wants and needs as you do about anyone else's.
- Fear less what others think and fear more the consequences of living by what others think.
- The cost of being boundary less erodes your self worth.
- Epigenetics has proved that if you change your biography you can change your biology.

**The only people who get upset about your
having boundaries, are the people who benefitted from you
not having any! JM**

**"You get what you allow and boundaries
teach people how to treat you" JM**

6. YOUR SELF-WORTH IS YOUR NETT WORTH. HOW TO "FEEL FREE TO BE ME"

There's a reason why self-confidence, self-esteem, self-love, self-respect and self-worth all start with "SELF". You can't find them in anyone else. Yet we often seek it and rely on it for external validation from the outside world. In fact we are placing the responsibility of our value upon others determined by the way they view us rather than how we view ourselves. In doing so, we diminish our value and disempower ourselves because we either always question or doubt ourselves and don't know our own true value.

A. Case study: Jo's "people pleasing"

If I look back at the brutal truth of my own choices in relationships including the one with my mother, I pretty much did whatever it took to be loved. With my mom, I kept trying harder by doing more to please her. Yet even when I did achieve a "not enough" response would follow e.g. I would get 80% for school marks, she would say, "Where is the other 20%? You just need to work harder and don't be lazy." When I got into the hockey B team she said, "You can get into the A team – just apply yourself." There were many other belittling comments.

In relationships, I tolerated behaviours that were unacceptable – basic disrespect and disregard for the things that are important to me and values I hold dear. They were sometimes people I wouldn't ordinarily feel comfortable to introduce to friends let alone my mother. The friends I had in my youth and the people I am surrounded by now reflect where I was and where I am now and they are worlds apart. It was more important for me to fit in than to stand out. I wasn't confident or robust enough in my being to stand alone and be unique or unusual, because I might not fit in or belong in a group.

My first marriage was a classic case of my settling for less than I deserved and less than what was true for me. I had never been married, I had just turned 40 and so many people would say, "What's a nice girl like you doing still single?" That rang the note in my head of: "There must be something wrong with me." The harder I tried to settle in a relationship, the more it seemed to elude me. I tried so hard to be whatever the guy at the time wanted, regardless of whether it was right for me. If it was someone who loved watching rugby at a local pub on a Saturday afternoon or going for drinks on a Friday night after work, I did it to fit in. Even though drinking at a pub was not my thing, it would be an evening I endured to fit in with the in crowd or at least so I could say I had a boyfriend.

After enough washed-out relationships (I called them three-month hit and runs), I was at such a low and couldn't understand what I was doing wrong when I was trying so hard. I kept thinking, Why is love so hard to find when it should be easy? I am not a bad person ... so what was wrong with me?"

Until one day, I sat down after yet another failed attempt at a relationship and sobbed in despair with one of my ex-boyfriends. He suddenly realised that under all my layers and frivolous façade, I was a deeply sensitive person, with a real need to be loved by someone who genuinely cared about me and not what they could get out of me.

This was a loud lesson in self-integrity: being authentic and honest with myself first. If I was not honest with myself how was I showing up for others? I was attracting what I was projecting.

That was a rude awakening. When I spoke to my life-coach about it, he said, "Jo, if you don't value yourself enough to be who you truly are, how do you expect anyone else to do so? It all starts with YOU not them. The more you define your value based on others' acceptance of you or not, you will continue to erode your own value till you completely lose who you are."

The foundation of self-worth is built on the value you place on yourself and is reinforced through consistent commitment to live your truth.

B.   Task: Self-Assessment:
Assess yourself below to see where you rank your self-worth
on a scale of 1 – 10 (1 lowest – 10 highest)

    a.   Practise self-acceptance.
    b.   Practise self-improvement.
    c.   Practise self-responsibility.
    d.   Practise self-assertiveness.
    e.   Practise self-integrity.
    f.   Practise living a purpose-filled life.

REFLECTIONS TO START BUILDING ROCK SOLID SELF-WORTH:

a.   Think about the ways you're currently trying to prove your worth. Do you try to earn love in relationships by putting others first? Do you push others forward at work? Do you determine your value by what you produce, achieve and do? Write down the ways you try to prove your worth at work, at home, with relatives, or with friends.

b.   Imagine what it would feel like to love yourself unconditionally – to know your worth instead of thinking you had to earn it. What would it feel like in your body to have love and appreciation in your heart, just for you? Close your eyes and really feel what that would be like, and then make some notes on what comes up for you.

c.   Think of the person you love most in the world, or someone who you feel is 100 percent worthy of their desires. Now, turn that love back on yourself, and imagine loving yourself and seeing yourself that deserving. What would you have togive up to love yourself unconditionally? What beliefs about your unworthiness would you have to release? Write down any thoughts that come to mind.

d. Imagine yourself being your own best friend and personal cheerleader. Give yourself the pep talk you would give a friend about how his/her hopes, dreams and vision are worth going after. Tell him/her what value he/she brings to the world Write it down for yourself as the compassionate, caring, encouraging and patient friend that you are to others.

Truisms:

- You attract who you are. Your vibe attracts your tribe.
- Your value does not decrease based on someone's inability to see it.
- Don't lower your vibration because someone else is unable to raise theirs.
- Your worth is not determined by the opinions of others.
- Be strong enough to let go and wise enough to wait for what you deserve.

"No one can make you feel inferior without your consent".
Eleanor Roosevelt

7.   MANIFEST IT ALL

One of the biggest stumbling blocks to creating change and taking action in your life is belief. No matter how much others may support you, or believe in you, or tell you that you can do whatever you set your mind to do, unless you truly believe in yourself, you'll fall short of achieving your desired greatness. Unfortunately, belief cannot just be imagined or expressed, it must be nurtured so that when you're called, you're ready to take action. Beliefs – like self-esteem, confidence and courage – all have their roots in self-worth, and until you own your worth and your inherent right to achieve more, believing in yourself remains elusive.

A.   *Case Study: Jo's Testimony*

This is where the truth of this book lies. I believe in what I am sharing because I am living proof of it. I told you in Chapter 1 that all I ever wanted was to be settled in a loving relationship with a family. As you have journeyed through the book with me, you saw how this was eluding me. I had read books including The Secret on how to manifest your dreams and could never understand why this was not working. Think of your dream as a seed – it has to go through a process of nurturing and nourishing with sun, water and compost to breathe life into it. So fuelling your dream with clear focus and elevated or positive emotions is what brings it to life. You have to believe in this process for it to come to fruition. As Dr Wayne Dyer used to say, "You have to believe it then you'll see it," not the other way around.

How do you create the belief you need to fuel your dreams?

Firstly, simply tap into your FEELometer. When things FEEL RIGHT, they ARE RIGHT and when they don't, they aren't. So when you are focusing on what is NOT feeling right, all you are achieving is FEELING MORE "NOT RIGHT" and getting more of what you don't want.

In other words, you are giving airtime to what is not serving you. You are fuelling it with energy to continue, gain momentum and keep yourself THERE! What you focus on expands, so choose carefully and mindfully to what you are giving energy and time. Where energy flows, energy grows.

B.   *Actions to fuel your manifestations*
   a.   You may have spent years people-pleasing and putting others' needs first, as I did. Which means you might not even know what it means to believe in yourself. Therefore, if you could be the support system for yourself, in the way you are for others, what would you do if you truly believed in you?
   b.   Believing in yourself may need consistent reinforcement so it becomes a new lifetime habit.
   c.   Most people who struggle with believing in themselves are focused solely on their past mistakes. So, instead of always focusing on your mistakes, failures or missteps, identify one to three circumstances in your life where you felt confident, knew you had the capability to take action and, when you did, the outcome was great. Write them down.
   d.   To stay connected to the belief that you can do anything, you have to anchor back into you. Begin each day by taking your own emotional temperature before anyone else's. Ask yourself: What do I feel, think, want or need? Start right now and write down what arises, and anchor that by committing to your needs before others.
   e.   THEN ask yourself: Is this taking me TOWARDS or AWAY from MY DREAMS and DESIRED DESTINY?
   f.   At any time on your journey when life takes you back into feelings that are not serving your future, recalibrate with your authentic/truest self so you remain focused and committed to the path you have created.

g. Cultivate and galvanise a mantra that you can call upon to tap into a bigger belief in yourself that can dissolve your doubts and fears. This will build the muscle of belief so you trust that whatever steps you take are moving you closer to your personal goals.

h. Commit to a daily morning practice/ritual like revisiting your goals, intentions, values, purpose or mission that will keep you committed, focused and moving forward towards your desired and well – deserved dream life.

i. Create a daily mind–set – a mantra or affirmation or guided meditation focusing on something positive to set the tone for the day. So you have a solid foundation to build on throughout your day so no matter what comes your way – you go back to YOUR TRUE NORTH.

C. **Truisms:**
- Life is not a dress rehearsal.
- You live the consequences of living someone else's dream, not them.
- Live with "at least I did" rather than the regret of "I wish I had …"
- Only YOU have the master key to unlock the possibilities hidden inside you.
- Use your fear constructively to propel you, not paralyse you, into your powerful new direction.
- There are no mistakes only lessons.

"What you think – you create. What you feel – you attract. What you imagine – you become. It's all up to YOU." JM

"Your stumbling blocks are your stepping stones to success."
Magic Johnson

ACCOUNTABILITY TO YOUR FEARLESS FORMULA

Now have completed your seven steps, pause and take a step back. Reflect on where you began in Step 1, on who you were and where you are now, and see what has changed or evolved and what you have learned about yourself. Take this time to remember the courageous journey you have chosen and the brave steps you have taken to prioritise you, build your confidence and self-worth and celebrate the incredible YOU that has emerged – rediscovered.

    a. Consider how far you have come and take a moment to honour that journey.

    b. What did you learn about yourself that you will take with you on your road ahead and what will you leave behind that no longer serves you?

    c. Have your goals changed (because you have changed)? And if so, what are they now? Write down these reflections.

Remember that the single biggest stumbling block to creating change and taking action in your life is belief – most of all belief in YOURSELF. Unfortunately, belief cannot just be imagined or declared, it must be cultivated and nurtured CONSISTENTLY, so that when you're called, you're ready to take action.

How will you hold yourself accountable to YOUR COMMITMENTS TO YOU? Whom will you choose to support you in your journey? Who has your best interests at heart?

"YOU are entirely up to you!" JM

"Be who you want to be not what others want to see!"
Unknown

Truism:

You are the pilot on your flight to freedom. It's been a long road of blood, sweat and tears. Ultimately it was worth it. Nothing worth fighting for comes easily. That's why we value it more. Knowing the work you have done to get here makes you value YOU more.

You have all the navigation tools at your fingertips:

- You have awareness of where you have been and the price you paid for it.
- You have awareness of what is possible and what awaits you to take.
- You have skills and tools to draw on and now need to commit to using them.
- You have your own inner guidance system. You only have to listen to it: when it feels right it is right and when does not, it's not.
- Your answers and insights are inside, not outside, you. Remember when you listen to the voice of others you bear those consequences, not them. Be careful what/whom you listen to.
- REMEMBER, where your focus goes energy grows. Choose what you focus on.
- Lastly this is not going to be a silver bullet to Nirvana. It requires commitment, practice and discipline, because changing your life is THAT important to you. No one else is going to do it for you. When you stumble, get up, don't give up because you didn't get it right. Recommit and continue, that's how superstar athletes win the Olympics. It's not easy and sometimes not pretty but the goal is the highest priority that fuels them to the finish line.
- Remember when you have learnt the lessons that are currently present for you, that the next ones will show up. Your work is never finished. However, your evolution and growth is ongoing and ever expanding you into all of who you are here to be.

Remember fellow traveller, YOU hold the master key to the rest of your life. It is a decision away. What are you going to do with it? Are your investing or disinvesting in yourself? Regret is a high price to pay and a ghost that will haunt you.

FLY HAPPILY!
FLY HEALTHILY!
FLY PEACEFULLY!
TRUST THE UNIVERSE AND TRUST YOURSELF!
BE TRUE – BE UNIQUE – BE FREE

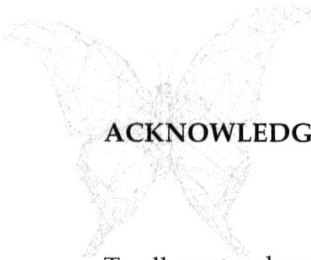

ACKNOWLEDGEMENTS:

To all my teachers – who hurt me and healed me – I thank you for helping me become who I am so I can help others through writing this book. My life has been rich in lessons and blessings and I am grateful to you all for my personal growth.

To my real mom, Marlene – thank you for being the mother I always wanted; for loving me unconditionally and encouraging me to be all I can be and to write this cathartic book.

My beloved tribe who have loved and supported me through my life's roughest roads as well as this journey to authorship. Thank you for your encouragement and for understanding the importance of my mission to pay it forward, to those who need it.

To my guardian angels (who are in Spirit) who have walked the road of life with me and helped me find my way – I am here because of you.

To my incredible mentor and writing coach Sarah Bullen, who kept me on track when I was getting derailed. She encouraged and course-corrected with patience and commitment to my end goal. Sarah also pushed me beyond the limitations of my mind and I am so grateful. My wonderful coach Kick-Butt Kate Emmerson, who kept me moving forward when I was disheartened and knew how to nudge me out of my myriad of emotions, that surfaced along the way, especially on the day I wanted to "burn the book".

Both of you held my hand lovingly and patiently all the way to the finish line – I couldn't have done it without you!

To Paula Marais who tightened and polished my book – thank you so much for understanding what the story needed for it to become its best version.

To Megan Barber for her patience and taking the time to understand me and translate that into such a meaningful cover. Thank you for bringing the year-long manuscript into its best version.

To my fellow authors who have been part of our "Writing Room", thank you for sharing that sacred butt-in-seat time, that enabled me to focus and persevere, knowing we are all in the trenches together and there to support each other to the end. My gratitude to you all.

And to you my reader, thank you for choosing my book as your stepping stone, to enable you to change your life, so you can live it the way you have always wanted.

REFERENCES:

Author	Year	Title	Publisher
Dr Wayne W Dyer	(2001)	10 Secrets for Success & Inner Peace	Hay House USA
Dr Christiane Northrup	(1995)	Women's Bodies Women's Wisdom	Piatkus Books Ltd
Louise Hay	(1994)	Heal Your Body	Hay House USA
Robin Sharma	(2002)	The Saint, The Surfer & The CEO	Hay House USA
Davidji	(2017)	Sacred Powers	Hay House USA
Dr Joe Dispenza	(2012)	Breaking the habit of being Yourself	Hay House USA
Dr John F Demartini	(2002)	The Breakthrough Experience	Hay House USA
Deepak Chopra	(1994)	7 Spiritual Laws of Success	Amber-Allen Publishing & New World Library
Don Miguel Ruiz	(1997)	The 4 Agreements	Amber-Allen Publishing
Eknath Easwaran Mountain	(2007)	Bhagavad Gita	Blue of Meditation

www.ingramcontent.com/pod-product-compliance
Lightning Source LLC
Chambersburg PA
CBHW071215090426
42736CB00014B/2828